# LIVING ON THE EDGE

## Stories of Inspiration

## Rabbi
## Dovid Goldwasser

The Judaica Press, Inc.

ISBN 1-880582-67-8

Cover Design & Typography: Zisi Berkowitz

For Library of Congress information, please contact the publisher.

THE JUDAICA PRESS, INC.
718-972-6200     800-972-6201
info@judaicapress.com
visit us on the web at: www.judaicapress.com

*Manufactured in the United States of America*

# מכתב
## מאת הגאון המפורסם פאר דורינו
## ר' אביגדור הכהן מיללער שליט"א

ב"ה

כבר נתפרסם הרב דוד גאלדוואסער במעשיו הרבים כאיש הרוח מדריך בני אדם בדרך התורה, ועכשיו מוסיף גם בחיבורו זה ללכת בדרכו לעורר ולעודד ולפחת נשמת חיים בקרב רבים מבני עמנו. יצליחהו ה' בכל מעשיו ויפוצו דברי השפעתו בישראל.

נאום

אביגדור הכהן מיללער

*In loving memory of*

# MRS. DEBRA ROBINSON

לעלוי נשמת
## **גיטל יחט** ע"ה
## **בת ר' חיים שלמה הכהן** נ"י

*Dedicated by her children*
*Dovid Yoel Mayer* נ"י
*Raizel Faiga* נ"י
*Chaya Sara* נ"י

# TABLE OF
# CONTENTS

## The Past

## The Present

# The Future

# ACKNOWLEDGMENTS

In appreciation of *Maran HaGaon* Rabbi Simcha Wasserman *zt"l*, whose awe-inspiring life is forever with me. *Daitan alecha.* להבהל"ח to *Maran HaGaon* Rabbi Avigdor Miller *shlita*, whose *hashpo'oh* is felt wherever Jews are found. His inspiration and encouragement are ever-present.

To R' Aryeh Mezei and Bonnie Goldman of Judaica Press for the special *kesher* we have developed. Their hands-on approach and perceptive insights have taken the drudgery out of preparing a book for publication and infused it with a special enthusiasm. Their professionalism and *erlichkeit* is refreshing. May they have continued *brocho v'hatzlocho* in all their magnificent efforts *l'hagdil Torah ul'haadirah*. Thanks also to the Judaica Press team who helped produce this book including Barbara Weinblatt, Nachum Shapiro, Zisi Berkowitz and Chana Leah Hirschhorn.

To Martin E. Friedlander, Esq., an exemplary role model both professionally and personally for all to emulate. His keen interest and expert guidance in every aspect of this book are responsible for its publication. He is a unique leader whose vision for the future has guided countless individuals and organizations and has expanded Torah horizons beyond imagination. It is my privilege to have his partnership in so many worthwhile undertakings. May Hashem grant him, his wife Liba, and their outstanding family continued blessing, success and *simchas*.

To R' Zalman and Ruchie Robinson and their outstanding *mishpocho* for dedicating this volume. It is a source of great *chizuk* for me personally to have them as part of our *kehilla*. Over the years I have witnessed their multi-faceted acts of kindness which have greatly benefited our community. Their pleasant demeanor, friendly disposition, and genuine modesty are exemplary. May Hashem grant them the strength and ability to continue doing their wonderful *mitzvos*, and may they have much *nachas* from their children לאוי"ט.

In honor of Rabbi Yitzchok Asiel, Chief Rabbi of Yugoslavia and Rabbi Kotel Dadon, Chief Rabbi of Croatia, whose *mesiras nefesh* for Klal Yisroel knows no bounds. It is my *zechus* to be so closely associated with them. May we soon see the קבוץ גליות, when we will all be joined together in Yerushalayim *ir hakodesh*.

To Reb Chaim and Barbara Kamenetsky, pillars of *chesed*, whose legendary work on behalf of the klal serves as an inspiration to people everywhere from all walks of life. It is a privilege for me to know them.

To Reb Yankel and Thea Berkowitz and Reb Jerry and Barbara Weissman, for their staunch support and encouragement on every project. Their friendship has enriched my life.

To R' Eliezer and Gitti Allman for their selfless dedication to Klal Yisroel. The credit for my educational and outreach efforts overseas is due to them. They have opened their hearts to בני ישראל

# ACKNOWLEDGMENTS

אחינו and have affected countless lives for the better. I will never forget being in Bosnia during wartime, getting calls from R' Eliezer around the clock every day, just to check if everything was okay, and if there was anything more that he could do to be of help.

To Mrs. Sonjia Samokovlija, whose indomitable spirit has been responsible for rekindling the light of Torah in many communities in far-flung parts of the world. I am indebted to her for giving me the opportunity to spread Torah in places all but forgotten. May she continue to share her considerable *kochos* and talents with the klal with blessing and success.

To the following people for their support and encouragement in this project: Eliezer and Helen Appelbaum, Zev and Aviva Golombeck, Chazzan Ira and Alyssa Heller, Dror and Susan Kahn, Gary and Gittie Klein, Rabbi Moshe Kolodny, Leib and Linda Koyfman, Jonathan and Yehudis Lewis, Rabbi and Mrs. Zechariah Lomnitz, Rabbi Duvie and Feigie Neuhauser, Jeff and Jodie Resnick, Howard and Rachell Sirota Esqs. There are additional names of *tayere chaverim* too numerous to list—*chaverim kol Yisroel*.

Special thanks to Estee Katz for her untiring efforts on behalf of the klal.

To Mrs. Ethel Gottlieb, Feyge Holtzberg, Brenda S. Mevorah, Suri Ossey, and Layala Salomon for putting in many painstaking hours initially editing this manuscript.

To Mrs. Simi Eichorn for her untiring efforts on behalf of this book, seeing the manuscript through from its earliest stages. Her valuable suggestions and considerable knowledge have enhanced the pages of this book.

To Nachum Segal, renowned radio personality, a master of words and an eloquent spokesman for *Klal Yisroel*. It is a privilege to work together with R' Nachum for close to two decades. His unique talents and *kochos* have united people from all walks of life.

To editor Steve Walz of *The Jewish Press* for his wisdom, constant support, and encouragement. He is a powerful advocate for truth, justice, and unity. We are blessed that he shares his considerable talents with the international community.

Forever etched in my *neshomoh* is the *mesiras nefesh* of my beloved parents, *avi mori* R' Yitzchok *ben* R' Yeruchom and *immi morasi* Riva Tzirna *bas* R' Benzion ז"ל. May the example of their noble lives always serve as a source of inspiration and blessing.

To my dear in-laws, Mr. and Mrs. Ben and Esther Koval, who carry on the royal lineage of the distinguished Kovalenko and Fink families. May they merit much *nachas* from their children, grandchildren and great-grandchildren. ברכה והצלחה אריכת ימים ושנים טובות.

The Commentaries ask: Why is a woman referred to as an *eishes chayil*, as opposed to a different name?

The reason is because a woman is comparable to a חייל—a soldier. She guards her house from all evil and protects the blessings within. She is on duty night and day in every situation—a definition apropos to my *eishes chayil*, Hinda Chaya טלאוי"ט. To be sure, none of my work on behalf of the klal would be possible without her *mesiras nefesh*. May we merit much *nachas* from our dear children, Yeruchum; Eliyahu; Rabbi Chesky, Fayge and Yitzchok Holtzberg; and Dassy. May they always go בדרך שהנחיל לנו אבתינו הקדושים, and may we merit to see בנים ובני בנים עוסקים בתורה ומצוות לעולמי עד.

*Purim 5761*
Brooklyn, New York
*Hametzapeh l'yeshuah*

# INTRODUCTION

"הן עם כלביא יקום וכארי יתנשא" (במדבר כג:כד)

The people will arise like a lion cub and raise itself like a lion. Klal Yisroel (the people of Israel) is described in *Parshas Balak* as a nation which rises like a lion.

The Chozeh of Lublin asks the question: Why does the *posuk* (verse) first say that the people of Israel will arise like a lion cub and then continue "and will raise itself like a lion"?

The Chozeh comments that the beginning of the *posuk* signifies that Klal Yisroel will raise itself—even when it is in a weakened state—and then, when Hashem sees that we wish to elevate ourselves, Hashem will raise us up yet further.

Resilience is perhaps one of the most important characteristics that we as a people have been blessed with. No matter how many times through our dark exile we have been oppressed, our people have demonstrated an indomitable spirit.

In my travels throughout the world, I have been privileged to witness this extraordinary strength time and time again. I have recorded these experiences in the pages of this book as they have been such a source of encouragement and inspiration.

I will never forget traveling through Sarajevo at the end of the war in the Balkans. Destruction and devastation were all one could witness walking through the streets. Buildings crushed by bombs, and highways torn apart by shells. Thousands of people were homeless. There were limited supplies of electricity, food and water.

I went to see what was left of the Jewish community center. As I viewed the makeshift soup kitchen and ad hoc emergency distribution center for pharmaceuticals, I was approached by a member of the Jewish community, who asked me if I would like to see a miracle.

I looked at him in amazement. What kind of miracle could he possibly want to show me? But I followed him anyway. He led me up four flights of stairs and showed me into a room behind two huge doors. There were approximately twenty-five children from the community who comprised the Jewish school. As I talked to the children and their teacher, something was revealed to me. Throughout the entire horrific war, the Jewish school had continued its classes uninterrupted. These children—who went to sleep at night, not to the sounds of a sweet lullaby, but rather to the sound of exploding bombs and shells—had made it their *raison d'etre* to live like Jews. Before leaving, I stood at the door and took one last look at those children, and I realized right then and there that the *posuk*: "A nation that arises like a lion..." had come to life once again.

I saw the indomitable spirit of our nation in those precious *neshamos* (souls). In the *zechus* of the pure and innocent children may we see the imminent arrival of *Moshiach Tzidkeinu.*

# THE
# PAST

## Prague, Czech Republic

# FROM A DISTANCE

*"If you want to know a man,*
*ask who his friend is."*

—Talmud

*Over the years, I have been privileged to meet interesting people from diverse backgrounds: A taxi driver in Warsaw, a headmaster in Budapest, a caretaker in Kiev, a street cleaner in Jerusalem, a counterperson in Los Angeles, and the publisher of a secular magazine in New York City. The list goes on and on. Sometimes those who appear as ordinary people, in reality, live remarkable, extraordinary lives. It is those encounters—the exchange of ideas, the sharing and interlocking of heart, mind and soul—that make for the most special moments in our lives.*

*Our Chachomim (Sages) say, "Acquire for yourself a friend" (Avos 1:6). The word "acquire" connotes "buying." This means that friendship is so important, it is even worth buying in certain situations. Choni, mentioned in the Talmud (Taanis), cried out to the Almighty, "Give me companionship or give me death." It has certainly been the companionship that I have enjoyed the world over that has given me an immense sense of fulfillment.*

# FROM A
# DISTANCE

Whenever I speak to a crowd, I try to analyze the listeners seated before me. I like to figure out their concerns and needs and see what I may be able to offer them that would be most beneficial.

It was a particularly warm evening in Prague and I had just ended my speech before a large audience. I noticed, during my inspection of the crowd, that there was one man in the audience who was staring at me intently with what appeared to be immense curiosity and thirst for learning. However, he did not sit among the crowd but, rather, he stood in the furthermost corner of the auditorium with his arms folded across his chest. Following the lecture, many people gathered near the lectern to ask me questions. During the entire question and answer period—which lasted approximately forty-five minutes—the same man who had been sitting in the back now stood at a distance behind the group that had gathered. Although he seemed quite interested, he did not allow himself to get close to the crowd or to me. I wondered about him briefly and then dismissed it with the thought, "To each his own."

For the next few days of my visit, this scene would be repeated. At each lecture, I noticed this same man standing almost outside of the room. After I finished speaking, as people would express their personal thoughts or questions, he kept his distance. As much as I would have liked to befriend him, I was hesitant. On the last night before leaving Prague, I spoke about being sensitive to others and being able to feel another's pain, and the difficulty of walking alone in the world.

Following the lecture, the usual question and answer period commenced. Once again, I noticed this same man standing isolated from the crowd. As soon as the crowd dispersed, he made his way up to me and, with obvious reluctance, introduced himself.

"My name is Andre*. I wanted to tell you how much this evening's lecture spoke directly to me. You see, when I was a little boy, our entire community was rounded up and told to meet at Umschlag Platze, the place of deportations. Little did we know that the trains were destined for the death camps. We had been told that we were going to a place where there would be a better quality of life. I trudged through the streets with my mother and when we were only two kilometers from Umschlag Platze, my mother, with a panic-stricken look on her face, shrieked, "We are getting too close— we are getting too close." With that, she instructed me to run with her away from the path. We eventually wound up in a neighboring city and hid there until after the war. Since that time, I have been plagued by the fear of ever coming too close to anyone. However, after this evening's lecture, this fear was replaced with a different one—the fear of leaving this world a lonely, friendless soul."

* The names in the story have been changed to protect the identities of people involved.

After a lengthy, heart-to-heart talk, I had the immense privilege of shaking Andre's hand—something that he had not experienced in over fifty years.

Andre's loneliness caused me to ruminate on how tough it is to go through life alone. Perhaps the most powerful source of positive energy is the strength one derives from close friendships. Indeed, it has been stated that two loyal friends are mightier than the angel Michael.

We fortify each other in more ways than can be enumerated: physically, mentally and spiritually.

A commonly used expression when a Book of the Torah has been completed, or on other momentous occasions in life is, "*chazak, chazak v'nischazeik*" (be strong, be strong and you shall be strengthened). Why do we say this?

One of the reasons we say this is because whenever we finish a section of the Torah, there is always the challenge to begin anew and not rest on our laurels. It is specifically at this crucial juncture that words of encouragement are vital.

I once heard a wonderful story about a mountain climber who dreamed of climbing an extremely high mountain. After much planning and training, he set off. However, he incorrectly estimated the amount of effort and energy he would need for the trek. Then a violent snowstorm erupted. The sub-zero temperature began to freeze the mountain climber's weakened limbs. Frostbite began to set in. With each step, the mountain climber feared that he would succumb to the elements and be buried in a snowy grave. Finally, the moment arrived when the mountain climber felt his last ounce of strength ebb. He took one more step and felt that it would be his last. As he lowered his foot, he felt something underneath. He bent over and brushed the snow away from the object. He was astonished by what he saw. A fallen mountain climber lay beneath the snow! His initial impression was that the body was lifeless. Upon closer examination, he detected a faint heartbeat. He knew that the only thing to do was to start rubbing the body to try to stimulate the man's circulation. After a few minutes, he saw signs of life beginning to return to the frozen mountain climber. However, a strange thing occurred. Not only had he revived the fallen climber, he had revived himself as well, due to the body warmth that was created.

Human warmth and friendship are two powerful sources of positive energy. Sometimes it takes a long while to realize this—it took Andre more than fifty years to realize the riches he had been missing.

# Budapest, Hungary

# INNOCENT BOOKS

*"You must not refuse to lend a book, even to an enemy, for the cause of learning will suffer."*

—*Rabbi Yehuda of Regensburg, Germany, 1200*

# INNOCENT
# BOOKS

We all dream of the day when there will be world peace and everyone will dwell together in harmony. Although in each generation we talk of achieving everlasting peace, we have yet to develop the one crucial ingredient necessary for peace—acceptance and love for all of G-d's children.

Textbooks are filled with detailed histories of wars and crimes against humanity. These atrocities have not only spanned the millennia, but have occurred everywhere in the world.

As a young boy studying in school, I took particular interest in world history, war and peace. I learned that attempting to understand the dynamics of people hating people is complex. However, what was utterly impossible for me to grasp was what transpired on that fateful night in history we have come to know as "Kristallnacht."

On this night the Nazis confiscated *seforim* (holy books)—innocent books—and set them ablaze in massive public bonfires. Etched in history are the countless scenes of those books and Torah scrolls set aflame and the shuls that were vandalized, pilfered and finally burned to the ground. The term "Kristallnacht" describes the shattered glass that blanketed the streets—the sole monument to the shuls and Jewish-owned stores that are but a glimmering memory.

Although none of us can ever comprehend the rationale of senseless hatred, I always wondered how one could ever hate books so much so as to let the flames of rage devour them?

◆ ◆ ◆ ◆

The State of Israel presented one of the important leaders of the U.N. with a special gift. It was a Passover Haggadah bound in a sterling silver cover. The book was personally inscribed by the Israeli Head of State. This U.N. leader was a rabid anti-Semite, but had hidden his true colors for many years. Following a dramatic ceremony in which this man was presented with the book, he returned to his office. He promptly and unceremoniously flung the book into the waste basket.

*Passover Haggadah presented at the United Nations.*

Later that night, as a maintenance man emptied the waste basket into a larger canister, he noticed something glimmering. He retrieved the object, not quite sure what it was. He opened the book and, after seeing the inscription, realized what had transpired. The book was then given to me by two wonderful people who wanted my assurance that the book's sanctity would be protected forevermore.

# New York City

# SPARING THE ROD

*"The holy writings shall not be made
impure by hands touching them directly."*

—Mishnah Yadayim 4:6

# SPARING
# THE ROD

nna\*, a European woman in her late 60's, works as a nurse, and is a dedicated professional. In fact, she was a G-d-send during the months in which my mother, of blessed memory, was ill. Anna devotedly assisted my mother each night during her last months on this earthly world.

I would travel weekly to spend time with my mother. During these visits, whenever Anna would be present, usually in the evening, she would ask me questions. The inquiries would invariably be about the beliefs and philosophy of the Jewish people. Her questions were varied and interesting. However, I always sensed a deeper reason for her inquisitiveness.

On the evening of my last visit, I remember her approaching me rather apprehensively. "Could I ask you to pray for me?" she timidly asked. "Of course I will," I told her. She then asked if I would remember her, to which I answered her by saying, "I will never forget what you have done for my mother."

\* The names in the story have been changed to protect the identities of people involved.

*Grave of tzaddik, Rabbi Shimon Oppenheim.*

Seven years passed since that last visit. I was on a lecture tour throughout Eastern Europe. It was during a brief stay in Budapest that I prayed at the grave of the holy Sage, Rabbi Shimon Oppenheim. Aside from my personal and communal petitions, I prayed that if there was anything that I could do on behalf of the *kedoshim* (martyrs) of the Holocaust, that G-d would deem me a worthy *shaliach* (messenger).

Immediately upon my return from visiting the cemetery, I received a telephone call from my eldest brother informing me that Anna, my mother's former night-shift nurse, wanted to get in touch with me concerning an urgent matter. When I contacted Anna, she explained that she had something in her possession that did not really belong to her. She had been meaning to return it for quite some time. Although she didn't reveal what it was, I gave her my address.

A few days later I received a package in the mail. I carefully removed the wrapping and stared at a brown box embellished with soft colors and peaceful, smiling angels. This strange looking case seemed to belong much more in a cathedral than in my own hands. As I opened the case, I was shocked. Inside lay an outstanding antique silver *yad* (pointer), similar to those used to help read the Torah when it was unrolled in synagogues the world over. As I gently lifted the religious article from its "case," I took note of its decorative stones, immediately realizing its high monetary value, aside from its inherent religious worth. This was obviously an antique; there was no question about it. There were even a few empty spaces which had apparently held other, perhaps more valuable stones in the past. This magnificent pointer obviously had a story to tell.

It suddenly dawned on me that I was so absorbed in admiration of this rare find that I had temporarily lost all awareness of how it ultimately had landed in my hands. Now, considering how I ended up with this extraordinary *yad*, its mystery grew even more. The questions racing through my mind knew no bounds: *How in the world did a non-Jewish night-shift nurse get hold of a* yad? *How long had it been in her possession? How old was the* yad? *Where did it originate?*

As my mind searched for clues to this unsolved mystery, so did my hands. Fortunately, it didn't take me long to find the following

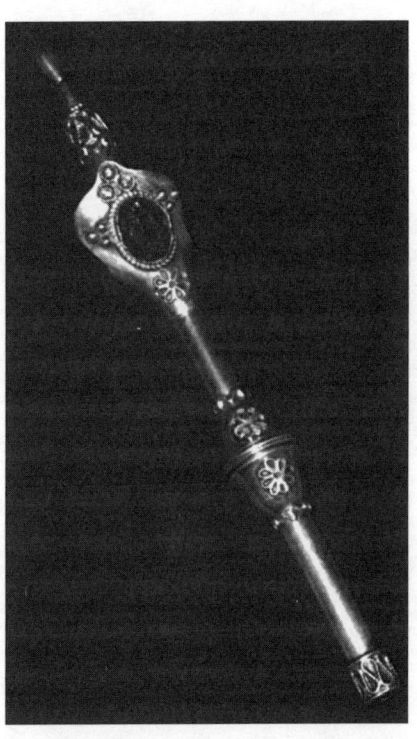

*Yad (pointer) saved from Kristallnacht.*

note hidden among the countless layers of tissue paper still in the cardboard box:

> *Dear Rabbi,*
> *I hope this letter finds you well. I've been meaning to give you*

*the enclosed item for a very long time. Please forgive me for not sending it to you before. This silver rod has been in my family for decades; it was originally taken from a burning synagogue on Kristallnacht. I always had a feeling you would appreciate this article. I hope I'm right.*

    *Anna Krautner*

# Lodz, Poland

# BY THE LIFE
# OF MY SON

*"He who closes his ears to the cry of the poor,
will himself cry out and not be answered."*

—Mishlei *21:13*

# BY THE LIFE
# OF MY SON

**M**eir* wore an anxious expression on his face as he hurriedly made his way through the narrow cobblestone street. A widower in his thirties, his mind was elsewhere as he headed home with his small packages. The bleak, unpromising sky, the cold—all reflected the tension and fear that clouded the lives of every Jew in Poland. Meir was one of the millions faced with a harsh reality—the Germans had invaded Poland. It was only a matter of time until the Jews of his beloved village would be forced to evacuate, perhaps be deported on those nightmarish trains....

Meir shuddered. As his mind quickly returned to his present surroundings, he noticed his dear friend Jacob walking towards him with packages of his own. As they exchanged quick glances, Meir took note of his friend's fatigued countenance. Signs of incessant anxiety pervaded Jacob's every feature. Meir shook his head in painful empathy as he thought of the overwhelming numbers of people, like Jacob, struggling to find the means for ensuring the sur-

* The names in the story have been changed to protect the identities of people involved.

vival of their wives and children. He then turned his attention to his own uncertain future. What should he do? Should he leave? Hide? These questions were becoming all too uncomfortably familiar...

As he concentrated on these troubling quandaries, Meir was about to turn into the private walkway of his house when he suddenly became aware of a familiar figure approaching him. It was Carl, a gentile neighbor of middle age. Although a simple man, Carl had proven himself to be a genuinely altruistic individual, constantly offering his time to take care of his fellow villagers' needs. Meir smiled and offered a warm handshake to his neighbor, curious to know why he had come. As Carl responded to the quiet greeting, Meir noticed that the man looked unusually tense.

Carl nervously cleared his throat, "I...er... wanted to know if I could speak to you," he whispered. "In private."

Meir's heart raced. Carl had never appeared before with such a dismal, apprehensive visage. What could it possibly mean? Did his neighbor know something concerning the war that he didn't? Was their village in immediate danger? Or perhaps Meir was just over-reacting. Perhaps Carl simply needed to borrow money. Once again, Meir's mind spun in circles as he led Carl into his modest home. Neither one of them spoke until they were both seated, each with a steaming cup of tea in hand.

Carl set his cup down and cleared his throat. As he proceeded to speak in a low, cautious tone, his eyes fixated on the table before him. "I'm sure you are well aware that while the Nazi regime is in power your people are in immense danger. It is no secret that their cruelty is harshest against Jews. We are all aware that the odds are against us. The Germans have already invaded Poland. It is only a matter of time until..." Carl's voice faltered. He paused, groping for the right words.

Finally, he turned and looked directly at Meir and heaved a deep sigh. "Meir," Carl whispered, his eyes overflowing with compassion, "Meir, there's no doubt in my mind that you are in terrible danger! *You will surely be killed!*" The words stabbed Meir's heart like a sword. "Your only hope is to hide. Let me take care of you; I know of an ideal place for hiding. I'll make sure that you have everything you need. Please consider it, Meir—it's your only chance!"

Meir was stunned. He had *davened* (prayed) for a *yeshua* (salvation), but he had never expected it to arrive through these means. Once again, a thousand questions flooded his soul. Why he, of all people? What about the rest of his beloved community? What of his home, his friends? Was it fair to be so selfish and fend only for oneself? Could he trust this Carl? Perhaps this was all a trap—after all, what was in it for Carl? Finding his voice, Meir finally responded, "Carl, I—er...I'm extremely grateful to you for your tremendous courage in trying to save me from danger...I... I'm actually a bit overwhelmed. But do you realize that by saving me you will surely be risking your life?"

"Yes," Carl answered firmly.

"And what about your wife?"

"I've discussed it with her. She's completely willing to help you in any way."

Meir furrowed his brow, thinking intensely for a moment. "This is a difficult decision. I need more time."

"Of course," whispered Carl, rising from his seat. As he turned to leave, he suddenly stopped, faced his neighbor, and added in a serious undertone, "I just want to advise you—the sooner you act, the better."

The next few days passed much too quickly for Meir. After hours of serious thought, consultation with his Rabbi and fervent prayers for himself and his entire nation, the decision was clear. It was his obligation to leave his work, his home, his entire life in the village—in order to save his own life. Meir also knew instinctively that it was imperative for him to abandon all external signs of his Jewish identity—to avoid attracting unnecessary attention. It was decided that he would disguise himself as a simple wood-chopper. His hiding place would be a tiny cabin in the thick of the forest. To Meir, this was the most painful transition in his life.

The actual move went unbelievably fast. Carl provided Meir with forged documents and swiftly transported him by wagon to the site of the tiny wood-chopper's cabin in the midst of the forest. As the wagon passed many Jewish homes, Meir gazed with a mixture of pain and longing. Would he ever see them again? What would become of his dear, dear friends? He felt his body shake in anguish out of fear for them.

As Carl quietly showed his friend to his new abode, he promised to come the following day to supply him with a few necessities. Once alone in his new dwelling, Meir sat down to absorb his surroundings. Except for the chirping of a few birds, it was frighteningly quiet. The simple structure surrounding him, the primitive lock on the door—all contributed to Meir's sense of vulnerability. His heart pounded in panic as he realized the extent of his weakness. His life was on the line, and all he could do was pray. Meir rarely felt as dependent on his Creator as he did now—or as close—he realized quite suddenly.

A shrill whistle broke Meir's train of thought, causing him to jump up involuntarily. The whistle was instantly followed by a long barrage of barking commands and mass marching. Meir felt his entire body on edge. He never imagined that he'd be so close to the enemy. Every movement, every sound shot arrows of trepidation to the core of his very soul. What was he to do? Where was he to run? Meir suddenly recalled his supposed savior, his neighbor, Carl. So it was a trap!

Yet something prevented Meir from accepting this last assumption. Carl simply seemed too sincere to stoop to such a base act of cruelty. Meir heaved an exhausted sigh. He was too fatigued to think straight anymore....

Just as he had promised, Carl came the next day. He brought bread, jugs of clean water, and a small supply of potatoes. Carl's face quickly grew pale as he listened to Meir's account concerning the nearby troops. Shaking his head, Carl assured him in a broken voice that as long as Meir disguised himself well, no one would harm him. After all, what would German soldiers possibly want with a poor wood-cutter?

As Meir regarded the clear signs of worry and frustration on his neighbor's face, his suspicions swiftly vanished, and he immediately regretted ever having doubted such a righteous man.

Yet as the days turned into weeks, Meir's fears loomed larger. Why should this gentile be any different from the Nazi soldiers? What would prevent Carl from handing Meir over to the enemy? With every whistle, order, and march Meir's anxiety snowballed into a never-ending frenzy. So unbearable was his overwhelming sense of fear and helplessness, that one day Meir could no longer tolerate it, he had to express his feelings to Carl. When Carl noticed Meir's tense face and nervous demeanor, he asked him what was bothering him.

"I just know it. You're like everyone else! You'll turn me in!" Meir cried, on the verge of tears.

Looking intently at his anguished neighbor, Carl responded in a steady, solemn tone, as if to impart eternal meanings to his words: *"I swear to you by the life of my son that I will never turn you in!"*

Meir froze in his place. Carl's words were so sincerely said that they had a dramatic, calming effect on his psyche. Immediately Meir apologized profusely and heaved an involuntary sigh of relief. He felt as if all of the tension that had been accumulating within him was quickly vanishing. Somehow, he had a powerful feeling that the worst was over.

Meir continued to survive in hiding, only now with a much more positive frame of mind. He quickly adjusted to his new life and mastered the art of filling his days productively by learning Torah from memory. When he felt himself unnerved with fear upon hearing the harrowing sounds of Nazi warfare outside, he knew to seek security and rejuvenation in his *Tehillim*, memorized years before. And Carl continued bringing him food and loyally being there for him.

Meir thus spent years in that same little hut, and only left at the end of the war. With Hashem's help, he managed to survive the tragic after-effects of the Holocaust, settling first in Switzerland and ultimately in America.

It was a number of years after Meir had established himself in the U.S. that he received the following telegram from abroad:

SON. STOP. FATAL ILL. STOP. HELP. STOP.

Confused, Meir looked at the address of the sender. In an instant, he fully comprehended the message and his eyes involuntarily welled up with tears. Dear, dear Carl, and now his only child was fatally ill! Carl, the man who had saved his life while risking his own....

Lost in a sea of nostalgia, Meir recalled the years of tireless devotion his neighbor had sacrificed to secure his safety and well-being. Images of Carl's regular visits, always accompanied by genuine words of comfort and encouragement, flashed through his mind. In those few moments of recollection, Meir relived those long, seemingly endless years in hiding, fully appreciating the impact of Carl's powerful expression of courage that had allowed Meir to survive and now enjoy the irreplaceable gift of life.

Overcome with a surging flood of *hakoras hatov* (gratitude), Meir immediately took charge of the situation and used his practical gifts for the sake of heaven.

In a flash, he found out exactly what Carl's son needed and telephoned his medical contacts in America. The correct antidote was immediately sent to Poland through a courier.

The following weeks passed interminably for Meir, who could only wait anxiously for news from Carl. Communications in Europe in the years after the war were not easy. Carl evidently did not have his own phone. The cheapest mode of communication available to him, at that time, was the telegram. Meir worried that perhaps the unspeakable had occurred before the medicine arrived. Meir vigorously shook his head to drive away the terrible thought that had so rudely entered his mind. He couldn't even bear to consider such a tragic possibility. After all, this was a perfect opportunity to repay Carl for all of his extraordinary kindness to him.

Finally, after what seemed like decades, the day arrived—a day that would forever be etched in Meir's memory. The long anticipated telegram was finally delivered, this one heart-warming like no other:

SON. STOP. HEALTHY. STOP. THANK YOU. STOP

Meir felt his heart sweetly rejoicing. In his hand lay a message he had been longing for ever since that nightmare called World War II. For years he had *davened* for the opportunity to reciprocate the remarkable act done by Carl. Song, dance and the purest praises to

Hashem flooded Meir's soul, for he had personally experienced *hashgacha pratis* (Hashem's Divine intervention) and His ability to mete out justice in infinite perfection. And nothing could ever possibly produce more joy than that.

# Szendre, Hungary

# IN THE FACE
# OF THE S.S.

*"To be Jewish is to invent hope where there is none."*

—*Simon Wiesenthal, Holocaust survivor
and famous Nazi hunter*

*Preparing the deceased for a* levaya *(funeral) is a true act of* chesed shel emes *(loving kindness). Not many people are eager to accept this awesome responsibility. But, when Kurche was only twelve, his father, who headed the* Chevrah Kadisha *(Burial Society), was out of town. There was no one to perform the service for the town's beloved communal leader so the young boy carried out the ritual in his father's stead. It was not easy for him to handle the corpse, but Kurche steeled himself, stifled his fear, and managed to do everything properly, just as he had been taught by his father.*

*Our fathers and grandfathers grew up very quickly in the old country and did not have much time for childishness or even childhood. They would need this extra measure of maturity more than ever during the Holocaust. Following is Kurche's amazing story.*

# IN THE FACE
# OF THE S.S.

When I was eighteen, in June 1944, the Nazis didn't so much invade, as they walked into Szendre, the town in Hungary where I was born, and quickly emptied it of virtually every Jew. Most of the relatively able bodied men were dispatched to a labor camp and that included me. I was tall and strong. The rest—my father, mother, and sisters were sent somewhere else. I had no idea where they were sent, but I knew it was unlikely I would ever see them again.

It was probably because of my Aryan looks—I was blond and blue-eyed—that the commandant chose me to be a supervisor. My responsibility was to choose those who would comprise the work crews. I paired the young and strong men with the old and weak to increase their chances for survival under the brutal conditions. Sometimes, the work would consist of carrying rocks the size of boulders with their bare hands from one end of a field to the other, without being allowed to pause for even a second to catch their breath. By the end of the day, a certain amount of rocks were expected to be lying on the other end of the field—all for no apparent reason.

After a few months, I noticed that almost every week there were different Jews, new faces, in the work battalions. The original prisoners were being replaced by new arrivals. It did not take long to figure out what had happened to the original prisoners. It was clear that it was only a matter of time before it became my turn. It was a *chesed Hashem* and a miracle that I had survived until now. The next moonless night, I decided to take my chance.

Knowing the terrain of the camp like the back of my hand, I escaped into the nearby forest. Then I began running. I ran faster than I ever thought I could, even though I was exhausted from the heavy labor and malnourished. All I heard was the crunch of leaves as I continued to run deeper and deeper into the woods. Soon my breath grew short and I knew I would have to slow down, but I didn't want to. Suddenly, I collided in the darkness with something, and fell to the ground. At first I thought I had knocked into a tree. But there standing in front of me was a man. I became paralyzed with fear, but could not utter a sound. I lay still, unable to make out the man's features. He silently stood over me. Finally, the man said in Hungarian, "Who are you?" I did not answer. The man pulled me and roughly dragged me through the leaves a little distance farther into the forest where there was a campsite. Dawn was beginning to break and I realized, with intense relief, that I had bumped into partisans. As soon as they saw my ragged labor camp uniform no explanation was necessary as to who I was...

The partisans offered me what food they had—berries and fruit they had found in the forest—and I ate what I could. Days passed, but I never felt safe. My situation, I knew, was precarious. The S.S. would surely search for their escaped prisoner, needing to make an example and deter others. The partisans, too, seemed uneasy with my presence and I knew they would prefer if I left. One partisan mentioned that he had found the uniform of a Nazi cadet lying on the ground the week before and took it back with him. I tried it on—it fit perfectly. In fact, they said that with my blonde hair and blue eyes I could easily pass for a German, so the partisans devised a plan. I would wear my new uniform and go to S.S. headquarters, a few miles away, and enlist. Perhaps from the inside I would be helpful in sabotaging the Germans. I accepted—I felt I didn't have any other options. I could not stay where I was much longer.

I couldn't believe how easily the bored bureaucrat who sat at the desk in the S.S. enlistment office accepted my story of having been separated from my regiment. As he shoved the application forms in front of me, he barely glanced up. The war was almost over, the Nazis were being bombarded from all sides and desertions were becoming more and more commonplace. The S.S. were gratified to find any able-bodied young man wishing to join. They were not too particular, so without any problem I became Hans Molner.

My first assignment was to guard the main road leading from Frankfurt to Rothenberg while a group of about five hundred Jews was marched to a labor camp thirty miles away. S.S. guards were posted along the way to ensure that no one escaped or tried to rest. I took up my position. The group came toward me, dragging their feet. Men, women and some children were prodded and shoved by the guards. I was filled with pity and felt tears in my throat, but I could not allow them to rise to my eyes. I watched, composing my face in a stern expression, as familiar and dear features and faces of my people passed before me. I needed colossal strength to stand by the side of the road and not offer help to an old man who stumbled, or to lift into my arms a child who wailed piteously, or to offer words of encouragement to a humiliated young man.

Then, as I looked down the road at the people who continued to march past, I felt myself reeling with shock and disbelief. There, about ten yards away came a figure all too familiar to me. I recognized him immediately by his erect and proud bearing—even under these horrendous conditions. I couldn't believe it, but coming directly toward me was my father! As he walked closer I saw him glance briefly at me—no smart Jew would stare directly into the face of the S.S. I then saw his expression change, but only for a millisecond. I continued to stare, riveted, into my father's face, and I never discovered from what fountain of resources I drew not to run and grasp him in my arms with relief. I saw the flicker of recognition in my father's eyes and I acknowledged it by silently pleading with my eyes for understanding. Then the procession passed and my father was gone.

I could only imagine what my father thought seeing his own son—the son he nurtured and taught—his companion and right hand, now dressed in an S.S. uniform guarding fellow Jews with a gun. All I could do was hope and pray that he would understand.

Not too long after this the war ended and I was swept along into prison with the rest of the S.S. I repeatedly tried explaining that I was a Jew, but no one paid any attention. "You Nazis are all the same," one soldier snarled. "You'll say anything to save your necks!" Finally, I managed to wrangle an appointment with the officer in charge. I recounted my story, but the commander refused to believe me until the chaplain accompanied us under guard to the nearest synagogue. I went up to the podium and prayed the prayers of my youth with utmost feeling. Only then was I freed.

Glad to be alive, I was nevertheless devastated by my loss—like so many countless others. I assumed that my mother and sisters were

gone and this was later confirmed. I had seen my father alive, shortly before the war ended. I hoped with all my heart that he was still
alive. The short-wave radio continually announced the names of
those who were being sought by family and friends in various points
throughout Europe. I constantly broadcasted my father's name:
"Birchu Klein of the town of Szendre. Your son searches for you. If
you hear this message, write to this address." For months, I continued to call my father's name.

Finally one day, a telegram arrived, with a message from my
father. He was alive and would be joining me shortly! I was ecstat-
ic, but my joy was tainted by doubt and misgiving. Would I be able
to explain myself—what I had gone through and why I could not
have done anything to stop my father's suffering? Would I have a
chance to talk things over? I wondered constantly whether my
father would forgive me.

Ceaselessly I agonized over these thoughts until the day of my
father's arrival. Standing on the dock, waiting for my father's ship,
I saw him standing by the railing, and it tore at my heart. He seemed
to have shrunk from the tall stately man he had once been. My heart
pounded with excitement and anticipation. I wanted to run up the
gangplank and hug him, and cry together about all that we had
endured and lost. As my father walked slowly toward me, however, once again I restrained myself and kept my hands at my sides.
My father came up to me and, once again, he looked at my face for
a long time. The expression on his face was completely and utterly
loving. We did not say a word about what had transpired—not a
word of explanation, nor vindication was ever demanded, requested or required. We never even spoke of the time my father stared
into the face of his son and it had become the face of the S.S.

Babi Yar, Russia

# BABI YAR

*"Shall these bones yet live?"*

—Yechezkel *37:3*

*Yom Kippur eve is a time of profound holiness for Jews, perhaps one of the most somber days of introspection in the entire year. It is on this day that we present ourselves before the Heavenly Court and plead for another year of life.*

*However, on the Yom Kippur eve of 1941, one hundred thousand Jews never had that chance. Instead of going to synagogue, they were taken to the outskirts of Kiev in the Ukraine and into the desolate ravine of Babi Yar. There they were lined up and shot. Many were buried alive. Afterwards, there was of course no monument or other sign to mark the grave of these holy martyrs of Babi Yar. In fact, the Soviet government did all that it could to make sure that Babi Yar would be forgotten. After the war, with the spread of anti-Semitism between 1948 and 1953, the issue of erecting a monument was once again brought up and dropped. The first attempt to erect a monument had taken place years earlier. However, the ravine proved to be a stubborn place. After two days of tor-rential rain pelted its fertile ground, the earth became loose and clods of soil were let loose everywhere, as if the martyrs were calling out in protest. Bones became unearthed and washed into the town's streets.*

*Ravine at Babi Yar.*

*In 1957, the Ukrainian Central Committee decided to put a stop to all of the talk about Babi Yar. It was a simple solution — destroy it and forget all about it. This was to be the second attempt to erase Babi Yar from history. Engineers decided that the ravine should be filled with earth by means of a special pump. They built a dam across the edge of Babi Yar and had pumped into the ravine tons upon tons of water and mud. Finally, the ravine became a lake. The water in the lake was green and had a certain foul stench to it. The dam rose in height until 1961 and then on Monday, March 13th, it collapsed. At 8:45 in the morning, with what was described as an awesome roar, flood waters began to pour out everywhere — into the roadways, the subways, everywhere.*

*Once again, the bones showed that they could not, and would not, keep silent. As Hashem said to Kain after he committed murder, "The voice of your brother's blood calls out to you." Clearly the martyrs were calling out loud and clear. The local people grew superstitious and afraid of this eerie phenomenon. Many would say that because of the evil committed against those hundred thousand, the very earth was now seeking revenge for the souls snuffed out in their prime.*

*After this, through the intervention of diplomats and government officials, it was finally decided to leave Babi Yar as it is and erect a small monument marker merely stating how many died in this place.*

# BABI YAR

When I first visited the Ukraine, I felt a sense of responsibility to visit Babi Yar and pay my respects. I walked outside my hotel on a sunny June morning to the taxi stand to hail a taxi for the trip to Babi Yar. One taxi after another refused. They were unwilling to make the trip. Perhaps they still carried the fear and superstitions that had been part of the past. Perhaps they were afraid that they too might see the bones and be forced to face the harsh reality that human beings could sink to such a level where hate and prejudice are allowed to rule. After being refused for quite some time, a taxi actually stopped and as I put one foot inside, he asked me, "Where to?" and I said "Babi Yar." With that, he stepped on the accelerator and nearly ran me over while speeding off. I was determined, maybe now more than ever. I was ready to walk if need be, but I was going to Babi Yar. Finally, there was a taxi driver who agreed. He told me to hop into the back and didn't say a word throughout the journey.

Soon we arrived at Babi Yar, less than an hour from Moscow. The taxi driver did not drive up close; rather, he waited on the other side of the road and pointed out Babi Yar to me. As I walked from the car, he surprised me by calling out in broken Yiddish, "Please say a prayer for the members of my family that perished here."

It was difficult to fathom. On this site so much destruction had taken place. With each step I wondered what had happened on that particular piece of ground. As I said the appropriate memorial prayers for the taxi driver's family and for all of the martyrs who had perished, I was moved beyond words. As I circled the ground, I was reminded of Yechezkel, the *Navi*, who circled the valley of dried bones, and tears came to my eyes as I uttered the words of the prophet, "Shall these bones yet live?" I ask you.

I later talked to the taxi driver. He spoke little Yiddish and no English. However, he told me that other taxi drivers were anti-Semitic and weren't willing to take Jews to Jewish historical sites. Plus, some of the people were superstitious concerning Babi Yar and feared revenge from the many souls murdered during the massacre.

*Monument at Babi Yar.*

Auschwitz, Poland

# DREAM WEAVER

*"An uninterpreted dream is like an unread letter."*

—Talmud Brachos *55a*

*Our forefather Avrohom, world-renowned for his hospitality, was visited by three men. These men did not have the outward appearance of being righteous. Yet, they were angels in disguise, sent by G-d to deliver very important messages to Avrohom and Soroh.*

*The Biblical commentaries ask why it was necessary to send these angels masked in the form of human beings. Couldn't the angels have appeared as they were—in true angel form? The answer: their disguise teaches us that the angels amongst us throughout the generations are not easily discernible.*

# DREAM
# WEAVER

Mention the word "Holocaust" and a plethora of feelings are evoked. In reality, our minds and our hearts can never comprehend the mass destruction and crimes against humanity committed during the bleak years of World War II. This was a time of world upheaval, when people seemed to go berserk en masse. A time when civilized nations of the world turned their backs on the persecuted and remained silent to the cries of their brothers and sisters as they were being stripped of their dignity, abused, tortured, and, finally, murdered.

Yet, of those who survived the unspeakable horrors of that dark era, many emerged with their *emunah* (faith) intact. They went on to rebuild a world that, according to Hitler's heinous plan, was to have become extinct. It is incredible to note that the faith and inspiration to continue with life was drawn from incidents that occurred in the darkest moments. Some of these incidents are recorded on the following pages.

Yaakov*, a man in his late 60's, who introduced himself when I spoke in Chicago one year, related this story to me. He told me that when he was a teenager, he was separated from his entire family and deported to the death camp of Auschwitz. Aside from the unbearable, back-breaking work from dawn until late at night, the rampant disease, illness and unsanitary conditions, the greatest danger to Yaakov's life was the lack of food. Yaakov had neither the nutrition nor energy that his body needed. Day by day, Yaakov felt his strength ebb away. The hunger pangs intensified, seeming to reach inward to the core of his soul. Soon Yaakov became ill and felt that his days were numbered. He mentally prepared himself to accept his Creator's will.

Each evening, after Yaakov was finally allowed to lie down on the hard, cold wooden shelf that served as his bed, he would pray. He prayed that were this his final day on earth, his *neshomoh* (soul) would be pure enough to directly enter Heaven.

It had been a long time since Yaakov had dreamt. In fact, how could one even allow oneself to dream amidst the shadow of death? However, one April night Yaakov felt a hand opening his mouth. He felt as if someone was feeding him liquid foods. Yaakov remained still and in his dream he hungrily swallowed. Yet he didn't have the strength to rouse himself to consciousness and challenge the dream.

When he awoke the next morning, Yaakov feared that this dream was the first sign that he was becoming irrational. More than any physical danger, Yaakov dreaded losing his mind. So that day, he focused his thoughts entirely on maintaining his sanity. In the evening, before he went to sleep, he once again prayed that his sleep would be uninterrupted by bad thoughts or confusion. As usual, he fell asleep instantly and suddenly felt that hand once again, this time holding his head up slightly and pouring the liquid food into

* The names in the story have been changed to protect the identities of people involved.

his emaciated body. As he urgently swallowed, he struggled to break out of his sleep and dispel this taunting fantasy. However, he felt too exhausted, and finally gave up his inner struggle, entering into an even deeper state of slumber.

The next morning as he awoke, although he felt strangely stronger, he felt certain that his end was near, for it was well known what became of prisoners who went insane. That day he spoke to no one, too frightened of what he might say. As evening came, for the first time in years, he did not long to sleep. In fact, he was terrified of what the evening's sleep would bring. He went to lie down on the wooden boards and resisted with all his strength, but to no avail. He was so extremely fatigued sleep soon overcame him. And then it happened. The dream appeared once again—the hand sliding down his face, opening his mouth and feeding him the liquid food. Yaakov could bear it no longer. With his last ounce of strength, he broke through the bonds of sleep with super-human effort. He stretched out his arm and grabbed hold of the hand that was feeding him. He held on and finally woke himself up to the point where he was able to open his eyes.

To his amazement, there, standing before him was a young man. Was he still sleeping? Or was this a real person? Yaakov demanded, "Who are you? Why are you doing this?" The young man pulled back in fear, loosening the hand clutching at his arm. He placed his finger on his lips motioning Yaakov to be quiet. In hushed tones, he said, "Don't you know who I am? I am the son of Mr. Lang, the shoemaker. We will never forget how you honored us with your presence at my brother's wedding. It was usually beneath the well-to-do of the town to attend the wedding of such a poor family as ours. Only a small crowd had assembled, and my father was able to afford only meager festivities. You will never know how much my father cried as you entered the room ready to participate at the wedding! He couldn't believe that a man as important as you had actually cared enough to join him at the wedding. Until the day when the Nazis took my father away, he never stopped speaking of you. Here, in this sickening place, I was fortunate enough to get a job in the kitchen, which means that I am able to salvage a few scraps of leftover food from the pots and pans. When I saw you here and realized that you were starving to death, out of *kavod* (respect) to my father's memory, I knew that as you honored our family and encouraged us to go on, I must do the same for you."

There is a *posuk* in *Tehillim* that says, "Surely goodness and loving kindness will pursue me all the days of my life."

Using homiletic license, I personally interpret this *posuk* to mean that when one performs an act of kindness for another person, that act of kindness will follow the person throughout his life, continuously paying dividends. It is completely beyond our understanding to fathom the reward for even a single good deed.

*Entrance to the concentration camp in Auschwitz.*

# Gdansk, Poland

# THE GREAT ESCAPE

*"Your secret is your prisoner;*
*if you reveal it, you become its slave."*

—*Ibn Gabirol, Spain, 11th century*

*Jewish tradition teaches that one should never give up hope. A frightening question was posed during the Holocaust by a man who knew that the following day he was almost definitely going to be tortured and sent to his death. He asked his spiritual mentor, Rabbi Ephraim Oshry, whether suicide in such a case would be permitted. He advanced three reasons why he should be allowed to take his own life:*

*1. Shouldn't he be spared further torture?*

*2. He had good reason to suspect that he would be murdered in front of his own family; and*

*3. If he took his own life he would have a proper burial. If he was murdered, his body would most probably be simply dumped into a mass grave.*

*Rabbi Oshry explained to him that although he understood the merits of these points he would, nevertheless, be prohibited from taking his own life. After all, who can give up hope that a miracle would occur and that he would be saved? We must always remember that* yeshuas Hashem *(G-d's salvation) can happen as quickly as the blink of an eye.*

*This question was recorded in Rabbi Oshry's book,* Responsa from the Holocaust *(Judaica Press).*

# THE
# GREAT ESCAPE

Peter*, a man in his mid-60's, had lived in Gdansk, Poland for the majority of his life. During World War II he had narrowly escaped being carted away to a death camp. He now considered himself fortunate to be alive. He was tall and thin with gentle features and a refined and sterling character. Since the war had ended, he had lived alone and kept mainly to himself. There was so much locked away, so many memories he had from his life during the war, particularly his harrowing escape. It was as if he was afraid to reveal that part of his life—his sudden separation from his family and other horrific aspects of his early life were simply too painful to talk about.

Peter worked long hours at a nearby sweater factory. It seemed that his only recreation was when he and a couple of his childhood friends gathered together to reminisce about a world that existed long ago. With these friends, he felt secure. They were, in many

* The names in the story have been changed to protect the identities of people involved.

ways, like the family members he had longed for, but had lost years before during the war. On one of these visits with his friends, Stashik, an old friend from Warsaw, began, as he usually did, to recount the old times. For some reason, Peter was compelled to relate the story of his escape with more emotion than usual.

He described in vivid detail the small picket fence in front of his house, and the secret space underneath the front porch that served as his hiding place. Moments before he was to be taken away, an open wagon carrying bales of hay passed him. Instinctively, Peter knew that this was his last chance of escape. Soundlessly, he secretly crept on to the back of the wagon and hid himself between the bales of hay. Peter was not discovered primarily because of the confusion of the times, as well as the clatter of the horses' hooves and the howling wind. It was as if G-d had enclosed the driver in a sound-proof booth. Peter survived the Holocaust by living off vegetation he found in the woods and with the aid of a villager who had mercy on him and throughout the war continually helped him. Certainly, he was protected by the sheltering wings of the *Shechinah* (Divine Presence). As Peter ended his story, Stashik was transfixed. His eyes were brimming with tears. Peter's account still moved him although he had heard it in bits and pieces before. It released a fresh set of emotions and thoughts that Stashik had not realized he still possessed.

Stashik blurted out, "Peter, you must..."

Peter responded, "Must what?"

"You must write this story down, people need to know this story—it would be such a profound source of inspiration for everyone to be able to draw from your story. It's such a miracle—how you were saved in the nick of time! How you knew which vegetation in the forests you could eat! It's a fabulous story!"

Peter shrugged his shoulders and said it wasn't something that he could do. He explained how he didn't want everyone to know this about him. He was a private person and certainly wasn't a writer. Stashik, however, was now determined. He would not accept Peter's "no." He used whatever argument he could to press Peter into writing the story. But Peter refused.

It wasn't until Stashik's next visit with Peter that Stashik was successful. He had decided that all Peter would have to do was give Stashik permission to write the story. All Peter would have to do was check the final story Stashik wrote for precision and accuracy. Finally Peter agreed. Stashik had convinced him that revealing part of what had happened to him would help kindle a flame of hope in souls yet untouched by the horrors of the war and perhaps now dealing with challenges they thought they couldn't surmount. And so, Stashik began the difficult and painstaking task of committing to paper the spirit and soul of a survivor.

When Stashik completed the article, it was a moving, astonishing tale of survival against all odds. Stashik published the article in the local Warsaw newspaper. In no time, people began discussing the fascinating article. It was soon picked up by an international news service and eventually appeared in various newspapers around the world.

Halfway across the world, an elderly woman named Marianne, living in Chicago, sat down to her morning coffee. Following the same ritual she had carried out for years, she brought in her morning paper and while sipping her coffee, began perusing it. For more than fifty years, that paper had been important to her. Now that she didn't get around much, it served as a crucial link to the outside world. The paper afforded her a sense of connection with others.

With interest, Marianne read the English translation of Stashik's article that was included in her local paper. Line by line she felt herself becoming more engrossed. Soon her heart raced and her limbs began to tremble. She called the newspaper office and asked where the story had come from. They explained that an international news service had provided the story. Marianne called the news service and traced the story to Warsaw and to a writer named Stashik. She immediately phoned Stashik at his Warsaw office. Stashik detected the urgency in Marianne's voice, although he did not understand English well. And she spoke a broken Polish. He was able to surmise that this woman wanted desperately to speak to the subject of the article. Stashik provided the home telephone number of his dear friend and wished the woman a good day.

Minutes later, Marianne braced herself as she dialed the number in Gdansk. As she dared to hope for the first time in fifty years, Marianne heard the voice of her long-lost brother, Peter. She was shocked and euphoric at once! Half a century is a life unto itself. She had been told that Peter's escape attempt had been unsuccessful. However, when she began reading the article, she had heard her brother's voice; she knew from the vivid description of the house and its surroundings, as well as details about Peter's family members, that this could not be mere coincidence. The house and the family were the same as hers. Although Marianne had forgotten quite a bit of Polish, she could understand Peter, and brother and sister eagerly conversed.

Nothing in this world is coincidence. The heavens had determined that two lonely survivors—separated since childhood—were destined to meet once again in this earthly world.

# Jerusalem, Israel

# SIBERIAN ANGELS

*"The profits of compromise
are nothing compared to its losses."*

—Rabbi Yisroel Meir Kagan, Radin, Poland, 1839-1933

# SIBERIAN
# ANGELS

I never knew why everyone called him "The Cousin." But, even the mere mention of "The Cousin" evoked a sense of reverence within those who uttered or heard his name.

I will never, ever forget the first time I met "The Cousin." He lived in a small Jerusalem apartment with bare walls, minimal furniture, and a definite old-country atmosphere. When you entered his humble abode, you immediately experienced a sense of spirituality, of life existing on a higher plane. The Cousin would talk to his guests seated at a small wooden table, one of his few worldly possessions.

When I met The Cousin, he was in his early eighties and he sat slightly bent over. His face was white as snow and he had a soft white beard to match. His piercing blue eyes, thick eyebrows, and flash of a smile could imbue you with strength for years. When you gazed into The Cousin's eyes, it seemed as if they simultaneously smiled and cried at you. You could see the happiness he had experienced in his eyes, but you could also sense the pain and torture that this gentle soul had endured. It has been said that the G-d of men dwells in mirrors. But, the G-d of a *believer* dwells behind the eyes. When looking into the eyes of The Cousin, you had the feeling that

G-d was peering directly at you.

*The Cousin, in Yerushalayim.*

One hot August afternoon, as the sun was setting, I had the privilege of being in the presence of The Cousin. Lost in time and space, I sat entranced as The Cousin spoke about the unspeakable—his life and times in the former Soviet Union where he was taunted and tortured for only one reason—his adamant refusal to sever his connection to Hashem. Throughout history, whenever a government tried enslaving the soul, it always settled with shackling the body—The Cousin had his fill of shackles. He could give a dissertation on the maltreatment of prisoners. He had experienced firsthand humanity's animal soul and the barbarity it is capable of manifesting. He could fill Amnesty International's archives with his experiences, an endless roster of crimes against humanity. Yet, despite all that his eyes had seen, he remained undaunted, holy and pure as the glow of the heavens.

The Cousin looked toward me, his eyes almost pleading for understanding. Could I, so young a man compared to him, possibly be able to know, or feel his pain? Did I understand the strength of character that had maintained such steadfast faith? Would it be possible to transmit his self-sacrifice and *dveikus b'Hashem* and relate to The Cousin's mission in life so that I could help carry on his legacy?

The Cousin not only did not like to talk about himself; he was far too modest to speak of his heroic acts or reveal how he was a humanitarian par excellence. Also, he was not interested in other people's sympathy. Only one issue burned in his heart—furthering and disseminating the glory of G-d in this world. It was for this reason alone that he related the following incident:

In the Soviet Union, The Cousin adamantly refused to work on Jewish holy days. This was, of course, forbidden by the government. Nevertheless, The Cousin informed his superiors that he would be unable to work for two days, due to a foot ailment. They suspected the real reason—the forthcoming holy days. A KGB agent appeared at The Cousin's door and gave the following strict orders: "Since you claim that an ailment currently infects your feet, we understand that you cannot actually come to work. However, your hands are perfectly fine. Therefore I have brought you your accounting work. It must all be completed over the next two days. When you come to work on the third morning, please make sure to return it finished. I've been told to warn you that if this work is not successfully completed, the consequences will be severe."

The KGB agent turned, slammed the door and hastily left. The Cousin stared in shock at the huge file of papers left for him to complete. The Cousin was proficient at his job and, as he looked through the work, he surmised that this amount of work would take no less than a week to complete! How could he manage to complete this, when he would not permit himself to work for the next two days and the only time he could even attempt it would be the night before he was to return to work?

Yet even though life sometimes seems impossible, The Cousin was not dissuaded from his mission. He tried not to worry during the two-day holiday and he observed it with his usual devotion and enthusiasm. As soon as the holiday concluded, The Cousin took out his work and began what some would consider an exercise in futility. With tears in his eyes, The Cousin recounted to me that when he picked up his pen something strange occurred—his hand seemed to write faster than his mind could think—page after page was completed quickly. By the next morning he had finished the entire file! The Cousin exclaimed, "It was a *malach* (angel), indeed it was a *malach* who did the work in the merit of my sanctifying the holy day." When The Cousin presented the work to his supervisors, they stared in disbelief. They examined each page and found his work flawless.

The Cousin's real name was Yitzchak and, as was true of our forefather Yitzchak, he too spent time upon the sacrificial altar. Like his namesake, The Cousin spent years upon the altar of *mesiras nefesh* (self-sacrifice), until he was released and fulfilled his lifelong dream of emigrating to the land of his ancestors.

# THE
# PRESENT

# Frankfurt, Germany

# UP IN THE AIR

*"The world is like a wedding. Just as
it is the goal of weddings to unite a
bridegroom and bride, so it is one's duty to
unite oneself in this world with G-d."*

*—Rabbi Jacob Joseph of Pulnoe, 1780*

A good teacher is one of the most effective tools for raising a generation of upright, moral, and concerned youth. A teacher often can make or break a child.

As a sign of respect, one of our most exalted Sages, the Vilna Gaon—who lived in Lithuania in the 18th century—always stood when he encountered his kindergarten teacher. Many people commented to him, "You are so much greater than he! Why would you stand?" He would always answer, "I stand because this teacher had an astonishingly positive effect on me. I was launched into the world of knowledge because of his caring, sensitive personality and infectious enthusiasm!"

Our earliest impressions are sometimes our longest lasting.

For myself, it was not an easy decision to become a teacher. I was well aware that if I would become a tailor, for example, and botch a tailoring job, it would be simple enough to reimburse that person. The risks are not the same if one makes a mistake as a teacher. The results can be disastrous.

The Talmud mentions the example of one teacher who was doing a terrible job teaching and literally was turning children off from learning. The Sages advised him to change careers and become a shoemaker. I often quip, "The Sages told him, 'Leave these souls alone—go work on other soles!'"

# UP IN
# THE AIR

In striving to be the best teacher possible, I knew that concern for students had to extend far beyond the classroom. A good teacher is concerned about students' personal lives—their joys, their fears, their ups and their downs. A teacher should be available for a student long after graduation. This benefits not only students, but teachers, for it is always gratifying for teachers to witness their students' success, advancement, and personal moments of happiness.

One day I received a telephone call from Mr. Zeigfried* of Lugano, Switzerland. He excitedly informed me that his daughter, Faye, was to be married in two months. Because I was Faye's former teacher and mentor they wanted to fly me to Switzerland to participate in the *chasunah* (wedding). Noting my hectic schedule and myriad obligations, I thanked Mr. Zeigfried, offered him my sincere congratulations, but I told him that it wouldn't be possible for me to attend. After ending the conversation, I thought a bit about it and then returned to business at hand.

* The names in the story have been changed to protect the identities of people involved.

One hour later a messenger service arrived at my office, delivering an envelope addressed to me. I opened the envelope and saw a first class round-trip ticket to Switzerland. "What should I do with these tickets? How could I possibly go?" I suddenly remembered the story of the Vilna Gaon who always rose when he saw his kindergarten teacher. That teacher must have done much more than merely teach the curriculum. So, too, I felt a responsibility to do all that was in my power for this student who had encountered numerous challenges in her teenage years and had overcome many obstacles along the way to reach this point in life. I phoned Mr. Zeigfried, thanked him for the ticket and told him it would be my pleasure to attend Faye's wedding. At that point he said, "I didn't want to tell you earlier, but the young couple would have been extremely disappointed had you not been able to attend."

As the weeks passed, final preparations were made for my trip. I would remain in Switzerland for only twenty hours and would return immediately to New York. The flight was scheduled for Tuesday evening at 9 p.m. I allowed the usual one hour to drive to J.F.K. Airport at 6:15 p.m. However, due to an accident on the Belt Parkway, traffic was at a standstill. With no alternative, I sat and waited. I consoled myself—there was still plenty of time. However, as time dragged on and on, and with less than one hour to departure, I grew concerned. Motorists began to leave their vehicles, wondering when we would be released from this holding pattern.

At 8:30 p.m., traffic resumed to normal. I drove as quickly as possible and reached Kennedy Airport at exactly 9 p.m. I ran through security, leaving my overnight bag behind. I desperately explained to the clerk that there was a wedding party waiting for me and that I must make *this* flight. A security officer ran alongside me, trying as best he could to assist me. But, as I reached the gate, airline personnel told me that the plane had already departed and could not be brought back.

I checked every airline, and found that there was only one more plane leaving to Europe that evening, but it would land in Frankfurt, Germany. The travel agent said he could get me on that flight but that there was no connecting flight to Lugano, Switzerland. I had less than three minutes to decide before the flight to Frankfurt was to depart. It was a difficult decision. There was just enough time to get to the wedding with a proper connection. However, without a connection, I would certainly miss the wedding and waste a ticket and money that was sent to me for a specific purpose—not to mention the waste of time traveling across the ocean. As I was about to take a step back, I once again remembered the Vilna Gaon. What would his teacher have done? I knew right then and there that as long as that couple was counting on my being there, I must try everything humanly possible to get to that ceremony. The agent hurried me aboard the plane and I grabbed an available seat. The door closed behind me and the plane began to taxi down the runway. That evening I *davened* (prayed) with extra *kavanah* (devotion). Our destiny, I knew, is sometimes unknown.

Early the next morning, the plane landed in Frankfurt. As I deplaned, I ran into the huge terminal searching desperately for a flight to Lugano. After numerous inquiries, I found that only one airline had a flight into Lugano that would arrive in time for the wedding. All the others were not scheduled to leave until after the wedding was certain to be over.

As I approached the ticket counter, the agent asked to see my passport. Apparently he assumed I already possessed a ticket. I handed him my passport and my now useless ticket from New York. He, in turn, glanced at it and handed my passport to another agent in a back room. Immediately upon seeing my passport they began an animated discussion. After hearing that I did not yet have a ticket, the man at the front desk informed me that the flight was already overbooked. In fact, he told me that there were already twenty people on the waiting list to get on that particular flight. As I was about to faint, the man who had been holding my passport came up to the front desk with a broad smile. He said to me in a deep, bellowing voice, "Herr Goldwasser, it is an enormous honor for our country to have your presence. How long will you be here?" He sensed there was a problem as he looked into my face and asked if everything was all right. I told him all about my problem. He whisked the other ticket agent to the back and whispered something to him. Moments later, the agent returned, ticket in hand, and said, "I hope that this seat will be satisfactory for your honor." I thanked him profusely and asked for no explanations. All I knew was I was getting on the plane. As I ran to the gate, I noticed an assemblage of people who were wait-listed for the flight. I heard as airline personnel announced that there were no more seats for this flight—wait-list people were asked to return to the main terminal.

I boarded the plane and discovered that my seat was located in the first class cabin. I was greeted by both the pilot and airline attendants.

When I arrived, I found the father of the *chasan* (groom) waiting for me at the airport to whisk me to the wedding which was scheduled to begin immediately upon our arrival.

Our Rabbis have taught us that when we are confronted with life's vicissitudes we must take whatever steps possible to meet the challenge. The important thing is to do our part and make the *hish-tadlus* (effort) without becoming discouraged. It may not always be easy, but the potential outcome is well worth the effort.

Long Island, New York

# IT'S ONLY A DREAM

*"There's only one thing rarer in
sleep than to dream we are sleeping,
and that is to dream we are dreaming."*

—*Chassidic saying*

# IT'S ONLY
# A DREAM

A dream, the Talmud tells us, is one-sixtieth of prophecy. There is profound meaning in our dreams. They reveal our hidden thoughts and help us understand what's hidden in our subconscious. A dream can also be an escape from reality, a respite from our frenzied daily lives. Occasionally, however, a dream may even provide a clue or serve an important function in saving a life.

It was well past midnight on a particularly warm June night. Having had a busy week, I was intent on making sure that my sleep would be uninterrupted. As I drifted off, I became oblivious to the conscious world.

A few hours later I began dreaming, but the dream was frighteningly real. Psychological studies have shown the effect of this mental activity on the body. In fact, some clinical studies have demonstrated that, on occasion, people who dream that they have touched something scalding hot with their hand may actually begin to develop a blister. This dream was so realistic that I felt it could actually manifest a physical reaction.

I dreamt that I was riding in the passenger side of a car with a man whom I had never met. As he barreled down the highway, I noticed that his eyes had closed and he had fallen asleep. To make matters worse, we were quickly approaching a sharp curve in the highway. With the speeding oncoming traffic approaching from the other side of the median, I immediately shouted, "Wake up! Wake up!" However, the driver, whoever he was, lowered his head slightly and seemed to descend into an even deeper sleep. Desperately, I shouted the first thing I could think of—"Wake up! For G-d's sake, wake up!"

With those words, I woke up in a cold sweat. Somewhat relieved that I had been dreaming and was not actually in the car, I calmed myself with the words, "It's only a dream!" I looked at the clock on my night table. It was exactly three a.m. Needless to say, the dream was a horrific experience. I decided to give *tzedakah* (charity) and thank the Almighty that this event had not really happened.

The next morning, I bumped into one of my closest friends. He startled me by saying, "You'll never believe what happened last night. My brother called me shortly after three a.m. He was driving his car on the Long Island Expressway, returning from North Carolina. I guess the trip was too much for him and he fell asleep at the wheel. All of a sudden, he heard a voice screaming, 'Wake up! For G-d's sake, wake up!' Thank G-d he did! *Boruch Hashem*, he tricked the Angel of Death by executing a harrowing maneuver, steering his car around a dangerous curve on the highway. My brother—who as you know is not a religious man—instantly became a believer. He called me to ask if there was anything special that he should do to thank G-d for sparing him. I explained to him that it would be appropriate for him to donate money to charity."

I was stunned by my friend's story. I still vividly remembered my dream and was a little shaken up because of it. I related my dream of the previous night to my dear friend; we both were astounded. From that day on I knew, unequivocally, that I would be careful whenever I use the words, "It's only a dream."

## Jersey City, New Jersey

# TRUTH OR CONSEQUENCES

*"For thirteen years, I taught my tongue*
*not to tell a lie; for the next thirteen years,*
*I taught it to tell the truth."*

—*Rabbi Pinchas of Koretz, Poland, 18th century*

A man who had committed many sins, in particular, stealing, once went to a great rabbi and asked how he could repent.

The rabbi told him that his way of repentance would be to tell only the truth. From that day on, he was never allowed to be untruthful.

The man repented, and for a number of months he refrained from stealing. One day, however, he heard that there was a wealthy man staying at an inn at the edge of town. He could no longer resist temptation. He began walking across town in order to mark his target. As he was walking, one of his former friends saw him and said, "Yossel, where are you going?" Yossel recalled that he had promised the rabbi he would never tell a lie. So he told him about the heist he was planning. Then he quickly added, "But please, don't tell anybody." Then Yossel quickened his pace to make up for lost time. This attracted the attention of another onlooker, who stopped him and questioned him: "Yossel, where are you rushing to?" Yossel once more recalled the words of his rabbi and told the truth. He added, "Please don't tell anybody!"

In Yossel's line of work, timing is everything. So he hurried even more. After encountering another curious acquaintance and telling him the truth, Yossel realized that it was now impossible for him to commit the crime. Too many people now knew about his plan.

The great Sages have commented on the verse in the Torah, "Keep far away from a word of falsehood" (Shemos 5:9). Why does the Torah specifically single out the sin of lying, more than any other sin? This teaches us, according to Sefer Chassidim, that the root of all other sins is falsehood.

# TRUTH OR
# CONSEQUENCES

For sixteen years I have been associated with Nachum Segal, a New York-based radio broadcaster. He has given me the privilege of delivering a daily message on the radio stations WFMU (91.1 FM) and WNSW (1430 AM). There is one program, of the many that I have participated in, that stands out in my memory. I had been discussing the importance of the attribute of *emes* (truth) when, in the middle of the show, I received an emergency call from a frantic woman. After I was off the air I was able to take the call. I was instantly alarmed when I picked up the phone. The woman on the other end of the phone was breathless and sobbing, clearly in the throes of a heartrending emotional experience.

She briefly explained that she had been listening to the program on truth, and felt compelled to recount her incredible story. It was about an incident so profound that it not only forever changed her life, but also made strikingly clear the monumental importance of truth.

She lived on Staten Island in New York City, she said, along with her husband, a teacher, their seventeen-year-old son, and an infant son. The baby was seriously ill. Physicians had told the family that the baby desperately needed a blood transfusion in order to survive. The baby, however, had a rare blood type. Finding a donor with precisely the same blood type was going to be difficult, fraught with disappointments. But doctors offered the family a ray of hope—their seventeen-year-old son's blood tests confirmed that he had precisely the blood type needed for the infant's transfusion. The family was overjoyed! Their search for a donor was over. Or so they thought.

Anyone who has ever tried to donate blood to a blood bank knows their stringent policies. A donor must be in good health, weigh over 100 pounds and be over eighteen years of age. When the woman heard this last stipulation, she hesitated for only a fraction of a second. Naturally, their son would simply say he was eighteen, instead of seventeen! He was, after all, the perfect donor, and this was an emergency! The boy's father, however, wouldn't hear of it. He adamantly refused to let his son even consider lying about his age. His shocked wife was beside herself. But neither her pleas, nor the outraged responses of those who heard of his decision could sway him.

Unbelievably, a couple of days later, a donor from another source was found. The baby was able to receive the needed transfusion. Nevertheless, many people remained unable to understand the father's stubbornness. Yet, life went on for the family, and their baby, fortunately, began to recover. That same week—not long after the baby's transfusion—their seventeen-year-old son set out by car for upstate New York, where he was going to attend a convention.

The mountain roads were not easy to navigate. Many stretches of the road, such as the one the boy was driving on, had steep drop-offs, without guardrails. Driving was even more treacherous that winter day with icy roads. Suddenly, the boy's car hit a patch of ice and began skidding toward the road's edge. The brakes were useless on this patch of ice. No amount of the boy's frantic steering could prevent the inevitable. The car careened head-first off a cliff and plunged into the ravine below.

In that area of the mountains, one can drive many miles without seeing another car on the road. Divine intervention, however, is a truly remarkable thing. Lo and behold, on that fateful day an Emergency Medical Technician (EMT) was driving to the mountains where he had a summer home. When he saw the tail end of the boy's car plunge off the side of the cliff, he was at first convinced that he was hallucinating. Nevertheless, he immediately pulled over. Sure enough, there was the car he had seen, now lying in a crumpled heap below.

After radioing for help, he grabbed whatever medical supplies he had with him in his car and began the dangerous steep descent down the side of the mountain. He channeled all of his energy into reaching the boy while still maintaining his footing on the loose rocks and soil.

It took some time for the EMT to climb down to the accident scene. When he arrived at the car, he was amazed to find the boy still alive, although in critical condition. Thankfully, an ambulance arrived quite soon afterwards, and the paramedics were able to carry the boy out of the ravine and rush him to the nearest hospital.

The fast-working "trauma team" in the emergency room worked hard to stabilize him. His parents were called and they quickly made the trip to the mountains. When he was out of danger, his parents met with his doctor. The doctor expressed how much danger the boy had been in. He said they were extraordinarily lucky their son was still alive. The doctor explained that the boy had lost a lot of blood. He emphasized that the boy was in such danger that had he lost even one additional pint of blood, he never would have survived his accident.

One pint of blood. An average transfusion entails at least three pints of blood. If this seventeen-year-old had donated blood for his baby brother's transfusion that very week—as his mother had wanted him to—he would have never survived the loss of blood in his car accident.

A father's adamant adherence to the principle of truth, and his unwavering faith in Hashem to find another donor for his baby, earned this family the privilege of being able to watch both of their precious children grow up.

# Brooklyn, New York

# ALL IN A NAME

*"A man is called by three names:*
*the name given to him by his parents;*
*the name others call him by; the name*
*that he creates for himself."*

—Midrash

# ALL IN
# A NAME

I never prepare for interviews with journalists. Off the cuff, unprepared answers always seem more appealing. Little did I know that it would have been impossible to prepare for a recent interview. Months in advance, a reporter for a New York-based magazine had scheduled an appointment to interview me concerning my outreach work in the community. The interview was scheduled for 12:30 p.m. promptly in my office. By 12:00, photographers had arrived and had begun to set up their equipment. By 12:30, the interviewer, Jonathan Mann*, had arrived. After exchanging formalities and meeting one another, we sat down to begin the interview.

Jonathan was a skilled interviewer. He asked appropriate questions designed to create sparks of interest. We had just reached the topic of crisis intervention when suddenly there was a loud knock at my office door.

With an urgency in her voice, my secretary, said, "You have an

* The names in the story have been changed to protect the identities of people involved.

important phone call!"

I replied, "Please take a message, Miriam." With a frightened look in her eyes, Miriam responded, "Rabbi, I'm sorry, the man on the phone said it was a matter of life and death and that he must speak with you!"

I had a feeling that although many people make use of the phrase, "a matter of life and death" easily, here it was for real. I looked at Jonathan, and he nodded, making it clear that it would be all right for me to take this call.

As I put the receiver to my ear, a voice bellowed, "Is this the Rabbi?"

"Yes," I said and before I had a chance to say another word, he screamed out, "I'm taking my life—nobody cares. I can't live with the pain. It's over! It's over!"

I began to speak with the caller, trying to engage him in conversation. I calmly asked why he wanted to take his life. He responded that he had lost his job and his benefits had run out. He had no family and had a history of depression. To make matters worse, he had just received an eviction notice for failure to pay his rent. He could not imagine that he—once a productive member of society—would soon become a faceless, homeless man, wandering through the streets of New York. Life no longer seemed worth living.

I immediately offered help. I told him I could help arrange for food and a temporary place to live. I also discussed job placement programs. He interrupted me, "That would have been helpful a year ago—now it's too late. I don't want to be pitied by people!" He angrily said, "The help never came when I needed it. I can't take it anymore—I'm going to take all the pills in this bottle right now."

I calmly and sincerely begged him, "Please don't—it's at the darkest hour of the night when the dawn appears. Although all may seem black to you now, each day offers a new lease on life!"

For some unknown reason, this only enraged him. "So you don't believe me!" he yelled mockingly. "Okay, fine, I'm taking one pill right now."

Desperately I said, "Please don't, we're having a nice conversation—can't we just continue—you sound like you have a lot to offer."

After a momentary pause, he said, "You see—I took it—one pill—now I'm going to take the rest."

My mind, heart and soul raced for something to say that would stop the senseless death of a tortured soul. Racing against time, I said to him, "By the way, what's your name?"

He answered that his name was Reuven. I could hear wonderment in his voice. "Why is that important? Why do you ask?" he questioned.

"I'll tell you, Reuven. I asked because we believe that a person's name defines the essence of their being. Reuven was Joseph's brother. He saved Joseph's life and wouldn't permit Joseph to die in vain. In Jewish tradition Reuven is given particular recognition because it was he alone, of all his brothers, who realized the paramount importance and inestimable value of human life. Reuven is your namesake."

Reuven then answered me, his voice a little changed and a little curiosity in his tone, "Could it be so? Is that really what the essence of Reuven is?"

"Yes," I responded.

At that moment, I heard Reuven sigh. "I never knew it—I never even knew what my name meant."

I then took his lead and said, "Reuven, I would be happy to meet with you and discuss your name and how it connects to your soul." We spoke a few moments longer, and Reuven agreed to come to the office to meet in person.

As I wished Reuven well and ascertained that it was safe to end the conversation, I noticed Jonathan and the cameraman for the first time since I had picked up the phone. I had been completely absorbed in my conversation with Reuven. They were shocked— overwhelmed with emotion and scared beyond belief. Jonathan asked for a drink of water. He said that there would be no need to continue the interview. He already knew how the article would read.

As I mentioned earlier, sometimes one simply cannot prepare for an interview.

# Brooklyn, New York

# IN SEARCH OF JOSH

*"A precious gem lies in the dirt.
We have to lean over,
brush it off and take it with us."*

—Rabbi Nachman of Breslov

*In* Ethics of the Fathers *(4:13) it says, "Despise no one and reject nothing for there is no man without his hour and nothing without its place." Rav Yisroel, the Maggid of Koznitz, comments that the Hebrew word for hour (sho'oh) also connotes "turning," or "paying attention," as it says, "To Kayin and his offering [Hashem] did not pay attention (sho'oh)" (Genesis 4:5).*

*One should never say, "How can I possibly draw those who are unholy to the service of Hashem?" for there is no one without the ability to "turn"—that is, anyone can acknowledge Hashem at any moment and turn his or her life around.*

# IN SEARCH
# OF JOSH

A s any public speaker knows, there are many "do's" and "don'ts" governing public speaking and enabling the presenter to effectively convey his or her message to the audience. Some of these are simple etiquette tips; others are more hard and fast, cardinal rules intended to maintain a speaker's cool and confident manner. One of the foremost rules: Ignore all distractions.

Being somewhat a veteran of the podium, I was quite accustomed to such distractions as blinding flashbulbs, coughing spasms, and occasionally, wailing babies. However, none of my past experiences could have prepared me for one of my worst nightmares as a public speaker.

During a seminar at which I was one of the presenters, a young man abruptly slumped over in his chair and fell to the floor, amid cries of shock and alarm from those seated around him. At that moment, all rules governing public speaking were promptly disregarded, for this was too much of a distraction to ignore! I immediately identified the fallen man as Josh*—someone who frequently attended my lectures—lying prostrate at the feet of his horrified wife, Marilyn. As I rushed toward them, amateur diagnoses flashed through my mind. Could it be a heart attack or an aneurysm, *chas v'shalom* (G-d forbid)?

Much to my relief, by the time I reached them, Josh appeared to be coming around. His wife assured concerned onlookers that Josh was simply exhausted from working a double shift on extremely little sleep. The explanation seemed plausible enough and everyone, including myself, began to relax. After a few tense moments, the lectures continued as planned. The crisis had passed.

Although I didn't dwell on it, the incident surprised me. I had known Josh and Marilyn for three years. In fact, I had officiated at their wedding. They were bright, well-educated, and indeed, appeared to lack nothing. I had never known Josh to suffer from any health problems. Although he appeared fine physically, I did notice that he had become somewhat distant and withdrawn.

One can only imagine my shock when I received a frantic call from Marilyn, a few months later, informing me that Josh had been missing for almost two days! I listened carefully as she filled me in on the details of his disappearance.

"I thought he was just late returning from work, so I went to sleep, thinking he would surely arrive home soon. When I awoke the next morning, I realized that he had never come home! I'm frantic! Tonight will be the second night Josh is missing, and there are still no leads at all! Please help me! I just don't know what to do!"

I desperately wanted to help the tearful woman find her husband, yet I felt as though part of the story was missing. The unusual circumstances of Josh's disappearance set off alarm bells in my

---

* The names in the story have been changed to protect the identities of people involved.

head, and I asked Marilyn if there was any more information that she could possibly offer regarding Josh's strange disappearance.

"Oh, Rabbi," she cried. "I don't know how to tell you this! Josh sometimes has trouble coping with some of the everyday pressures at home and at work. He tried to find an easy escape, and he began experimenting with various drugs. He only meant to use them to relax a little bit, but before he knew it, he was hooked."

When I heard this shocking revelation, I felt personally responsible. Why couldn't they have confided in me? Why had I not been able to recognize the signs of substance abuse? Yet I knew that in so many areas of life, people become experts at masking their deepest problems, whether it's substance abuse, physical and emotional abuse, eating disorders, or a myriad of other problems.

The immediate problem at hand, however, was locating Josh. If, *chas v'shalom*, a child is missing, there are wonderful organizations such as "Child Find" that are called in to help. Whom does one contact to locate a grown man who has vanished? The police had already been notified, the community was informed to be on the lookout, and several groups were organized to help comb the New York City streets in search of Josh.

I dedicated myself completely to the search efforts. It was difficult for me to undertake anything else during this period. Troubling thoughts raced through my mind as to what might have happened—amnesia, overdose, or a drug deal gone sour. The possibilities were endless.

Four days passed since Josh's disappearance. Much to everyone's dismay, not a single clue surfaced regarding his whereabouts. With each passing hour, the chances of finding Josh safe and sound grew more remote. I contacted various people and organizations to pray on Josh's behalf. The search efforts intensified and fliers were printed with a description of Josh and a telephone number for any-one with information to call. There was even a reminder to *daven* (pray) for Josh's safe return written on the bottom of every flier. These fliers were distributed far and wide with many of them plas-tered on lampposts and bulletin boards throughout the city.

Four more agonizing days passed without a sign of Josh. He had been missing for over a week and some people despaired of ever seeing him again. It was close to midnight on Tuesday evening when my phone rang. As soon as I picked up the receiver, Marilyn, almost incoherent, shouted, "Josh called!! We know where he is! We're going to pick him up right now."

I'll never forget that call. The *tefillos* (prayers) of the entire com-munity had been answered. Josh was alive, on his way home! The next call I received was from an extremely soft-spoken Josh, thank-ing me for being there for him. The following day he revealed his incredible story to me. He explained how his drug habit had begun as a seemingly harmless way to take his mind off his worries. But the narcotics quickly tightened their grip on him until he was no longer in control. Despite his shame, an ever-increasing portion of Josh's days were consumed by drug use. He became despondent and disillusioned and eventually felt too ashamed of his addiction to remain in the community. He felt like he was a failure to both his family and community. Soon his pain felt too agonizing to bear. He decided to run away. Life on the streets, however, had become a dis-mal blur of drugs and depression.

On Tuesday night, Josh had been wandering the streets of Manhattan when he spotted a flier on a lamppost. Upon closer inspection, he realized that the flier depicted none other than him-self. He was stunned that so many people were praying for him. It sent a profound message to Josh—that he was worthy of people's prayers. He felt renewed faith in himself.

Psychologists have long sought to discover why some people develop addictions. One theory is that addictions develop to correct an imbalance. Addicts become trapped, unaware and unable to deal with their thoughts, emotions and actions. They may drink, eat to excess, or, as in Josh's case, take drugs, in order to disassociate themselves from their perceived deficiency. When Josh saw the flier, with its plea to pray on his behalf, it finally made him realize that so many people truly *did* care and that, even with his troubles, he was still worthwhile. He then understood, at long last, that it was time to come home.

Josh still had a long road to travel to wean himself from his dependency on drugs and deal with his real life situation. He knew that with a support group of people who really cared about him, he could do anything.

In fact, one-third of America's adult population has had a prescription for mood-modifying drugs filled by pharmacists in this country. Over the years, drugs have become more acceptable—even fashionable—and readily available. No one is immune to the world of drugs and no community can ignore this. The cause may be peer pressure, a difficult moment in life, or simply thrill-seeking. The evil inclination can skillfully use these tools to bring about someone's decline.

We have to be vigilant in our adherence to the admonition of "*v'nishmartem meod l'nafshosechem*—you should be careful to protect the physical welfare of your bodies." Drugs present a danger to people—physically, mentally, and spiritually. It is therefore of utmost importance to promote public awareness and drug education so that the community understands the serious issues that we face.

# Birmingham, Alabama

# BITTERSWEET

*"...from the strong comes the sweet..."*

—Shoftim *14:14*

# BITTERSWEET

One never knows in this world whether an omen is good or bad. Jewish tradition teaches us that "...from the strong (bitter) comes the sweet..." (*Judges* 14:14).

Within the plan of *hashgachah* (Divine Providence), the seemingly opposite attributes of *rachamim* (mercy) and *din* (strict justice) fuse to become one as friend and foe unite for a common goal.

"A blessing in disguise," is not merely a sweet-sounding cliche, it is a lifelong perspective that should be ever-present and never forgotten.

I have learned this repeatedly. But the story of what happened to two of my students serves as a perfect example of this.

Sharon* and Ben were students of mine and had kept close ties over the years. I was elated when they came to me and revealed that they were engaged to be married.

Before they would accept the traditional wishes of mazel tov,

---

* The names in the story have been changed to protect the identities of people involved.

they made me promise that I'd officiate at their wedding. I enthusi-astically agreed.

As they left my home, I thought to myself, "What a perfect cou-ple; both so giving and sensitive." There was no question that their marriage would be a wonderful asset to the entire community.

Approximately eight weeks later, I received a frantic phone call from Sharon. In a trembling voice she told me the following: Ben, being athletic, could never resist the invitation to play a game of bas-ketball. He had been invited by one of the local amateur teams to substitute for a player who was unable to make the game. As Ben was going in for a lay-up shot, he tripped, fell over and hit his head on the hardwood gym floor. Ben's head split open and he was uncon-scious. Immediately, he was rushed by ambulance to the nearest hospital. It was fortunate that that evening some highly skilled doc-tors were on call at the moment Ben was wheeled in. The doctors gave their immediate attention to Ben. While examining him, they discovered something quite unbelievable—Ben had a growth in the back part of his head which needed to be removed at once! Following hours of surgery, the chief of surgery emerged flashing the victory sign. *Boruch Hashem*, the operation had been a success.

As the days passed, Ben's recuperation went excellently. The doctors unanimously agreed that had the accident never taken place, the growth would have surely progressed undetected and taken Ben's life.

It has been sixteen years since that fateful encounter of *hashgacha* and *din* on the basketball court. An additional six chairs have been added around the table to accommodate Sharon and Ben's wonder-ful children, *Boruch Hashem*. To this very day, Sharon and Ben pre-pare a *seudas hoda'ah* (feast of thanksgiving) each year on the exact date of Ben's fateful fall.

Queens, New York

# ALL OR NOTHING

*People say: "Money is not found for important things. But it is found for unimportant things."*

—Talmud Chagiga

*Money, or the lack of it, can make or break someone. Certainly, the obsession with money can change a person.*

*A wealthy man lived in Poland in the late 1700's. Economic conditions were bleak, even beyond a depression. There were poor people living on the streets who were dying of starvation.*

*One of the most respected* tzaddikim *(righteous people) of the generation approached the wealthy man and asked for charity to buy food to feed the starving. The wealthy man, named Alex, politely refused. He said that although he was sorry, his money was presently tied up. Alex then offered additional excuses. Finally, the disappointed* tzaddik *pointed to the window and asked Alex what he saw through his window. Alex walked over to the window, looked outside and said, "Why, I see lots of people. I see little children playing, an old man walking and clutching his cane, and ladies returning from the market with their purchases."*

*The* tzaddik *replied, "Now come over here," and pointing to a mirror, instructed Alex to look into the mirror mounted on the wall. "Tell me, what do you see?" asked the* tzaddik.

*Alex, in a bewildered manner, answered, "Why, I see myself, no one else!"*

*At that moment, a smile appeared on the* tzaddik's *face. "Exactly my point, Alex," said the Sage. "A mirror is no different from a window, other than the fact that it has been covered with a sheet of silver. The same can be said about you. When you looked out the window, you were able to see everyone. However, once you became 'covered' with silver and gold, you became oblivious to everyone else."*

# ALL OR
# NOTHING

"Theft of any sort is corrupt. However, when it's an 'inside job' it is particularly violating." These were the words that Sarah* disclosed to me as she began to relate her problem.

"Al and I have been married a little over a year. When we returned from a week's stay at my cousin's house in California, we received a call asking if we happened to have seen my cousin's wallet that contained quite a bit of cash. It was missing and there was some important information written on a slip of paper inside the wallet. I asked Al if he had seen it, to which he replied in the negative. I thanked our cousins for their hospitality and went about my business.

"Two weeks later, Al and I were invited to dinner at my parents' home. The following morning, during my mother's routine call, she happened to mention that she couldn't seem to find her diamond

---

* The names in the story have been changed to protect the identities of people involved.

ring. Days later my mother told me that she had thoroughly searched the house and was sure that her ring was lost forever. I never connected these incidents until I went to the bank three weeks later to withdraw money from our savings account. I made out the withdrawal slip in the amount of $300. When I gave it to the teller, she looked at me and said that she was sorry but I did not have that much money; only $50 was presently in the account. I told her that she must be mistaken; I knew we had over seven thousand dollars in that account. The teller produced a printout which confirmed that $7,200 had been withdrawn over the past two weeks. I ran home in tears. When my husband finally returned, I asked if he was aware that $7,200 had been withdrawn from the account. He turned red and began to stammer. He said that I was not supposed to know about it and that he needed it for an urgent matter. He assured me that the money would be replaced. Al told me to trust him; he knew what he was doing. As time went on, I began to see how Al had gradually stopped paying the bills. It seemed as though any time there was a household expense, he always told me that he was broke." Sarah ended the story by saying, "Rabbi, you've got to help me. I don't even think he's going to work any longer."

I scheduled an appointment with Sarah and she said that she would attempt to convince Al to accompany her. Sure enough, the next day Al and Sarah were seated in my office. Sarah began to discuss the changes she perceived at home. Al, who had always been a good husband, now behaved erratically. After a long, heart to heart discussion, Al confessed, "I like to gamble a little bit, nothing heavy, just to pass time, like going bowling." We then discussed his "pastime" briefly.

However, when Al and Sarah went home that evening, Al broke down and confessed to much more than a "pastime." Al revealed that he had been gambling heavily for the past few months. In fact, he had missed too much time from his job because of it and had been fired. In addition, he owed an enormous sum of money to the wrong people. Out of desperation, he had resorted to "lifting" a few valuables. He reassured Sarah that everything would be fine in just a short while, it was just a phase and would pass in time. Unfortunately, as the weeks went on, it grew worse. Al would gamble at a casino until the wee hours of the morning and not return until the following day.

This time, Sarah literally dragged Al into my office. Al was unrepentant and said, "Rabbi, you don't understand. I just do it as a thrill. You have no idea how my adrenaline pumps when the roulette wheel is spinning, or the excitement when my number is drawing near, or when the cards are shuffled to begin a new game of blackjack." Al continued, "I have scored some big winnings, I just know that soon I will win enough for us to retire and then I'll quit this hobby forever."

I then said to Al, "Let's face it—we've got a problem." Pointing to all the things that had gone wrong, I quoted the statistic that one third of the members of Gamblers Anonymous had lost a job, 44% have stolen from their employers and one sixth have divorced. As I continued, it seemed as though Al was finally taking a reality check. Al emphatically stated, "I'm not going to any gambler's therapy group, so you can forget about that!"

After another super-charged session in which emotions were flying high, I finally got Al to agree to do two things: First, he would attend one meeting of Gamblers Anonymous, and second, he would pray for Divine help.

Are you wondering how I was able to convince Al to go to the Gamblers Anonymous meeting? Why, it was simple—I bet him two to one that he wouldn't go!

P.S. After months of attending the Gamblers Anonymous program—in addition to the couple's meetings with me—Al recovered and once again entered the workforce, cared for his wife and became a productive member of society.

Gambling addiction can happen to anyone. The desire to "get rich quick" can be overpowering. As it says, "*Ohev kesef, lo yisbah kesef...*" (*Koheles* 5:9)—one who loves money will never have enough money." The exhilarating thrill of a game of chance can be as addictive as a powerful drug.

Rav Yisroel Salanter once visited the home of a wealthy member of his community to discuss an important communal matter. A pile of money lay on the table in front of Rav Yisroel. While they were talking, the man was interrupted by an urgent message and needed to leave the room for a short while. When he returned, he found Rav Yisroel was gone. He searched the entire house but he could not find Rav Yisroel. When he opened his door to continue his search outside, he discovered Rav Yisroel standing outside. Rav Yisroel explained that he did not want to remain alone in the room with the money and possibly be tempted. Therefore, he thought it advisable to wait outside.

If the father of the *mussar* movement, Rav Yisroel Salanter, felt this way about money, we can only imagine how much more so do we—in our generation—need to guard ourselves from the pitfalls of money.

Johannesburg, South Africa

# LISTEN TO THE CHILDREN

*"By the sweat of your brow will you eat bread…"*

—Bereishis *3:19*

# LISTEN
# TO THE CHILDREN

One usually associates South Africa with lions, elephants, jungles and swamps. To be quite frank, up until recently, those were the first images that came to my mind. However, after a week's lecture tour through South Africa, I now think immediately of an inspired and enthusiastic Jewish community that left an indelible impression on me.

It was a cool summer evening. I was to give a lecture on the theme of truth in a very large auditorium in the center of Johannesburg. A huge crowd of people had turned out for the lecture, and additional seating had to quickly be arranged. There was literally not an inch of space that wasn't filled.

At the end of the hour and a half talk, there was an opportunity for the members of the audience to ask questions and have a private consultation. I don't remember all of the questions that were asked. They were the usual—a halachic inquiry about Shabbos, a question on the topic of truth, a question on the Torah perspective of a relationship....

There was, however, one question that totally shook me.

A young woman hesitantly approached me. She appeared to be unsure whether to ask her question or not. Finally, she lowered her eyes and asked if I thought her parents would forgive her if she died.

I was shocked. Many questions ran through my mind at that moment. Why was this young girl, who appeared to have her whole life in front of her, contemplating her own death? What morbid reality was she facing? Was she contemplating suicide? Was she on drugs? No child thinks of his or her own mortality, unless confronted by a situation that makes life seem precarious and fragile. Fortunately, Hashem gave me the right words to draw out her pain.

I asked her if she thought her parents loved her.

With intense conviction which showed on her face, she answered, "Yes, very much so," nodding her head emphatically.

"Parents who love forgive their children for many things, so whatever it is that is troubling you, remember that. Now tell me, why did you ask such a question?"

She explained to me that she was suffering from an eating disorder. Her physical health—her heart, kidneys and other vital functions—had deteriorated to the point that her doctors had warned her that her life could come to an abrupt end. She described, in horrifying detail, her downward physical spiral, and how slowly but surely her life was ebbing away. She then repeated her question: "Do you think my parents would ever forgive me if I died?"

I thought for a moment and then answered: "Knowing that your parents love you so deeply, it could be that they will come to a level of forgiveness. However, what I am not sure of is if your children will be able to forgive you."

The young woman, who up to this point had been lethargic and withdrawn, displayed keen interest. "What do you mean—my children? I'm not even married yet!"

I gently explained to her that we have been given the sacred mission of bringing children into this world. In Jewish mystical books it is said that under the *chupah* a couple is joined by the children destined to be born from the ensuing marriage. Hashem wants those children to be born. "I am not sure that the children that you, in the future, are destined to bear will be able to understand why they were not given their chance to live."

At that point, the young woman broke down and cried.

We discussed her situation for quite some time. Unfortunately, I have had a great deal of experience dealing with eating disorders so I was able to bring a lot to the conversation. In fact, at the time, my book, *Starving to Live*, a spiritual guide to eating disorders, was being edited. By the end of the session, she had agreed to enter into a new program for eating disorders that could help her gain a new perspective on life.

She revealed to me that that evening was a turning point in her life. The last I heard she was doing better and putting enormous effort into restoring her health.

We must realize, however, how many thousands are consumed and ultimately overwhelmed by this often hidden challenge, sometimes even forfeiting their lives.

# IN THE NAME OF PEACE

*At the end of every* kesubah, *we find the words "hakol shorer v'kayom—all is valid and confirmed." The word "v'kayom" also means "exists." The commentaries ask: If we have stated that all is legal, why do we need to add "and confirmed"? It has been suggested that the* mesader kidushin *(officiating rabbi) ensures that the marriage is legal and proper. However, it us up to the couple to continually work at their marriage, to ensure its success.*

127

*Recently* Sholom bayis *(domestic peace) has become a hot topic. Truth be told, it was probably always a hot topic, but nowadays people are ready to admit that every home has its challenges. With increased pressure today in the areas of finance, livelihood, children,* shidduchim, *and coping with an abundance of materialism, every family faces challenges. Sessions on preparing for marriage, interpersonal relationships, and parenting classes have become a must for today's generation.*

*Our Commentaries explain that if a couple truly feel* ahavah *(love) for each other, then they are able to overlook and ignore the shortcomings and quirks of their spouse. As we say in the* tefillos *(prayers) for* Yomim Noraim *(the High Holy Days),* "Al kol p'sho'im techaseh b'ahavah—*over all transgressions, please cover them up with love." This signifies our desire that Hashem, Who is All-Merciful, will forgive our transgressions because of His enormous love for us.*

*The* gematriya *(numerical equivalent) for the Hebrew word* ahavah *is thirteen, which is the exact numerical equivalent of the Hebrew word* echad, *which means one. Ahavah takes two different individuals, from diverse backgrounds and with distinct personalities, and molds them into one.*

# IN THE
# NAME OF PEACE

A couple entered my office one cold night in December. They had been married for a few years and now, they stated, they were deciding to call it quits. They felt they simply could not continue anymore. They proceeded to tell me that they seemed to be exact opposites. Each one brought with them their list of complaints—the things that the other person did that irked them and all the areas where each other's expectations had never been met.

I spent a considerable amount of time talking to them about the importance of *shalom bayis*. I explained how two people coming from completely different family backgrounds need to find ways to understand each other and be appreciative of each other's unique abilities. I emphasized the importance of having realistic expectations, setting goals and working together as a team. I also tried to convey the idea that basic ground rules should be established for mutual respect and honor. It was also suggested that the couple try a simple exercise each week to better understand the likes and dislikes of each other. Although they thought that my suggestions were helpful, they remained pessimistic.

As they were about to leave, I told them that the Baal Shem Tov has given us a "mystical charm" that a husband and wife may utilize when a marriage seems doomed. The Baal Shem Tov suggested that the couple take out their *kesubah*—the marriage certificate with which the couple was married under the *chupah*—and read it over together. It will surely have a positive influence.

The couple left the office. Approximately one hour later they called me. The husband and wife had proceeded to look for the *kesubah* and they found two similar looking documents that were used at their marriage. One of these was in actuality a *t'noyim*, an engagement contract, while the other was the marriage contract they were looking for. However, the husband and wife had then gotten into a heated argument over which was which.

I begged them to come back to my office so I could clarify for them which was the *kesubah*. They arrived clutching both certificates. I immediately showed them the proper document. However, I noticed that the wife's name written in the *kesubah* was different than the one which her husband used. I questioned the couple about this. They told me that truthfully the wife's name was the one that her husband used, a Yiddish name. The wife explained that the day before the marriage, a friend had told the young bride that you have to have a Hebrew name for the *kesubah* and suggested a Hebrew name to use. The wife stated that it was the only time she had ever used that name, and had long since forgotten about it.

I then asked the couple, who had already told me that they hadn't had a day of peace and tranquility since their marriage, what their relationship had been like before the day of marriage. They emphatically answered that their bond had been the strongest possible and they had truly and deeply cared for each other. However, since the time of their wedding, it had been downhill all the way.

Without hesitation, I obtained a new form and promptly wrote out for them a new *kesubah* with the wife's real Yiddish name.

Magically, the marriage began to come together and, for the first time in years, the couple learned once again to truly deeply care for each other. The couple kept in touch, informing me of their progress. I recommended that they go to a marriage counselor who would give them practical advice from a Torah perspective, which they did.

Who knows? One prays for *Siyata D'shmaya* (Heavenly assistance) in every area of life. Sometimes it comes in the form of the right connection, additional support, or an unusual coincidence. Sometimes, it comes with a revelation that is simply Divine.

Monsey, New York

# AN UNDERSTANDING HEART

*"Be the master of your will,
and the slave of your conscience."*

—*Chassidic saying*

*You see them dressed in rags, camped out underneath bridges, on the trains, or merely trudging down the street. They are sometimes elderly, sometimes middle aged, and sometimes even teenagers old beyond their years. As much as we may want to ignore them and pretend they don't exist, they are a reality of the world in which we live. They are the poor, the downtrodden, the less fortunate members of our society.*

*Humanity has been charged with a responsibility to be sensitive to human suffering and pain, to help lift the less fortunates' burden and do benevolent acts. Certainly, the suffering of the impoverished is difficult for many of us to comprehend. Many of us live in a world of excess. It's a yearly tradition, for instance, for hot dog manufacturers or other groups to run a contest during which young people wolf down up to thirty-three hot dogs, one after the other at record breaking speed.*

*Can we really understand the hunger pangs of a child sent out of the house early in the morning without breakfast? A child whose dinner may consist of crackers and a drink? Can we relate to a child who doesn't even own a winter coat? Who lines the inside of his lightweight jacket with newspapers to deflect the piercing cold whenever he goes out? Can we hear the silent cries of starving children echoing from the boondocks of Biafra to the swamp lands of Bangladesh to the hills of Jerusalem to the cold water flats of the Lower East Side of Manhattan, and beyond? Even in the war-torn cities of Sarajevo, Bosnia, and Herzogovina, machine guns may be the audible killer, but hunger murders in silence.*

*May our conscience never allow us to witness starvation and stand idly by.*

# AN UNDERSTANDING
# HEART

A pang of conscience inspired me to join a group of yeshiva students from Brooklyn who had been approached before Pesach one year by a relief organization for assistance. We were trying to raise urgently-needed money for the poor. We had been assigned to a close-knit Chassidic community fifty miles from New York City. The plan was to approach individuals there and ask them to contribute to this important cause.

On the designated day, we traveled to our assignment and things went quite well. We were gratified that sufficient monies were being raised. However, before returning to the city, my partner and I had one more address to visit. We climbed up a narrow staircase leading to the doorway and rang the doorbell. When the door opened, we realized that a terrible mistake had been made. One could easily see the shadow of poverty cast upon the entire house. The children were dressed in tattered and torn clothes, the wallpaper was peeling, the floors were worn out, the furniture was broken, and there was a general atmosphere of want.

The woman of the house asked us how she could help. However, before we had a chance to contrive an excuse, the woman had already scanned the brochure which we both held in our hands. Without even giving me a chance, she said, "I'm so happy that you've come! You are doing such important work." She asked us to wait a moment, disappeared into a back room and emerged a moment later with an envelope that she proudly handed to us. If there was ever a time that I could remember feeling ill at ease, surely this was it. As we thanked her for the envelope, she in turn graciously thanked us for coming. We said goodbye and left.

Once back in the city we opened the envelope that the woman had given us. We found food vouchers worth $10.00.

# Chicago, Illinois

# ANGELS IN
# THE NIGHT

*"A father is pained at the suffering of his children. Children are not so much pained at the suffering of their father. G-d is pained over our suffering. We are not so much pained over G-d's suffering."*

—*Rabbi Mendel of Kotzk*

# ANGELS IN
# THE NIGHT

What little girl does not dream of standing under the *chupah* (wedding canopy) at her wedding, beside her *chasan* (groom)? Every mother and father also dreams of the day that they will walk their precious child down the aisle.

In the Talmud, our Sages discuss the complexity involved in bringing about anyone's wedding day. After all, it is no simple matter to unite two different worlds. It was certainly no simple task for Mr. Katchen* to arrange for his daughter Sarah's wedding.

Sarah was an only child. She was a loving daughter, an excellent student with the *chein* (charm and grace) that all parents pray for in their child. She was indeed blessed. Sarah was the focus of Mr. Katchen's life, particularly following his wife's passing.

A lovely wedding was arranged for Sarah and her special groom. The wedding was to be held in late December on a Monday evening in Chicago. All the necessary arrangements were made—

* The names in the story have been changed to protect the identities of people involved.

flowers, photographer, engraved invitations, and excellent musi-
cians. Mr. Katchen took particular pride in personally overseeing
every detail. He intended to make sure that his daughter and future
son-in-law would experience such a joyful wedding, they would
remember it for a lifetime.

Although Mr. Katchen had constantly struggled to earn a living,
his daughter never went without anything. Many times, Mr.
Katchen would quietly deny himself things so that his daughter
could have a pair of dress shoes like the other girls, or pretty bows
for her hair. While she was growing up, thoughts of how he would
afford to pay for a proper wedding for Sarah concerned Mr.
Katchen. Fortunately, as a newlywed, Mr. Katchen had been given
an insurance policy by his company that he had been told was
worth several thousand dollars. It was this insurance policy that Mr.
Katchen intended to cash in to pay for his daughter's wedding.

The Friday before the wedding, Mr. Katchen went to retrieve the
insurance policy. It was kept in a small box that had been tucked
away for years. When he took it to the insurance company to be
redeemed, he received the shock of his life. The policy was now
worth only a few hundred dollars! It was Mr. Katchen's worst nightmare. How could he possibly tell his daughter that her wedding
would have to be called off? How could he live with himself if he
had to do this? His agony was unbearable. In desperation, he spent
endless hours trying to figure out what to do. He felt too ashamed
to call anyone for advice and reveal this terrible secret. Awful
thoughts crossed his mind, thoughts that no human should ever
ponder.

Mr. Katchen knew that he should immediately call the caterer
and ask him to cancel the wedding so that all the food and preparations wouldn't go to waste. However, being a man of intense

*emunah* (faith), Mr. Katchen could not abandon his lifelong belief in *nisim* (miracles). He decided that he would wait until the night before the wedding to tell the *kallah* (bride), *chasan*, all the guests, and finally the caterer that it would have to be canceled. Perhaps, he desperately hoped, G-d would perform a miracle at zero hour—what right did Mr. Katchen have to intervene and prevent such a miracle!

The next seventy-two hours were agonizing. Mr. Katchen couldn't eat, drink or sleep—in fact, he barely could breathe. His mind darted back and forth to when Sarah was a little girl. He reminisced about all of the wonderful years of her youth. Vivid images of all the happy, memorable times they had shared flashed across his mind. It was as though he had a photographic album stored in the archival recesses of his brain.

As Sunday night approached, Mr. Katchen realized that he would have to gather his courage and go to the caterer and tell him that the affair had to be canceled.

On the way to the caterer, as Mr. Katchen trekked through the snow, one additional thought plagued him far more than anything else. During his wife's last moments, he had promised her that he would take care of Sarah's every need. Now, not only would he not be able to face people in *Olam Hazeh* (this world), but he realized that it would be impossible for him to face people in *Olam Habah* (the World-to-Come).

He felt completely destroyed when he finally reached the catering hall and rang the bell. Mr. Sarna, a well known caterer and the proprietor of the catering hall, opened the door and ushered Mr. Katchen into his inner office. Mr. Katchen sat down. As he gathered his thoughts and reined in his sadness, he began, in a tear-choked voice, "Mr. Sarna, I appreciate all that you have done for me and my daughter. You have been extremely kind and professional."

Mr. Sarna abruptly interrupted Mr. Katchen and said, "Mr. Katchen, I know you're appreciative, but truly it was unnecessary for your cousin to pay me in full earlier this evening. You should realize that I certainly trust a man such as yourself to pay as is customary, at the time of the wedding. Thank you so much, but it was really unnecessary."

Mr. Katchen thought he must have been dreaming. "What are you talking about, Mr. Sarna? I don't have any cousins!"

With frustration showing in his voice, Mr. Sarna said, "Please calm down, Mr. Katchen. Approximately one hour ago, the doorbell rang and I went to see who it was. It was snowing heavily, but through the glass door I saw a man who appeared to be poor. He wore a long, torn, black coat and a crushed hat. On his face I could detect the impressions left by the ravages of time. Many such unfortunate souls come to our hall. I give them leftovers from weddings or other occasions. I try to send them home with at least enough food for a day or two. I assumed that this elderly man was here to collect food. I asked him to wait in the front hall, near the door, while I went to bring him a food package. In a quiet, genteel manner, the man explained to me that he had not come for food. He then explained that he had come to pay for your daughter's wedding tomorrow night. He said that he was your cousin, Mr. Katchen. He then handed me several thousand dollars, paying for the wedding in full. When I saw that he was paying in cash, I asked him to wait just one moment so that I could present him with a receipt. I went to my office just for a second, but when I returned, he had disappeared. I ran to the door, looked down the streets, but the old man had vanished into the night!"

Mr. Katchen broke down and spent the rest of the night weeping. He was so relieved, so baffled, so completely thankful. Whoever did not witness Mr. Katchen's *simchah* (joy) at his daughter's wedding has not witnessed true joy in their lifetime. Mr. Katchen never did discover his benefactor. This story was told to me by the caterer's son.

It says in *Psalms* (*Tehillim* 91:11) that G-d has commanded His angels to accompany us in all our paths. However, it does not specify whether the angels walk ahead of us, behind us, or by our side.

New York

# MEIR BEN CHANA

*"From the straits I called G-d and He answered me."*

—Tehillim *118:5*

*"A person cannot release himself from the house of detention"* (Brachos 5b). *Although our Sages say that a person cannot "release himself," Rabbi Yehuda Loewi, the Maharal of Prague, writes that regarding prayer we do not say a person cannot release himself, as it is Hashem who releases him.*

# MEIR BEN CHANA

The last place I thought I would find myself during the sacred period between Rosh Hashanah and Yom Kippur was at a huge federal correctional institute, one of the major penitentiaries in New York. Months earlier I had received a call from the popular singer Mordechai Ben-David. He revealed to me his plan of providing the Jewish inmates with inspiration and encouragement and suggested that we both go together during this special period. Mordechai would sing his soul-stirring Jewish melodies, and I would try to deliver uplifting words.

Much had ensued since our conversation. Plans were made; background checks were required; musical accompanists had to be arranged and transportation was organized.

When we arrived at our destination, we were all taken aback by the forbidding towering walls surrounding the sprawling prison complex. Yards of barbed wire stretched across fenced-in areas. Grey steel bars and iron grates were all that were in view. These people were surely excommunicated from the rest of the world.

After completing the initial application process for entry, we were thoroughly searched and required to go through a series of metal detectors. Belts and shoes had to be removed. Radios, calculators and anything electronic was not permitted inside the prison walls. We moved from one area to another with special escorts who stamped our hands with ink and supervised our every move.

Once inside the multi-purpose room where our program was to be held, approximately fifty inmates filed in. Despite their suppressed state and lack of freedom, we almost immediately established a warm rapport with the inmates. As the program began, one could hear a pin drop in the room. Despite the obvious distractions, every individual in the gathering listened with intense attention to every word that was spoken and every note that was sung. Spontaneous applause filled the entire room. Several times, the entire assemblage broke into singing and dancing.

The transformation of this forbidding maximum security prison into a chapel of prayer, filled with spirit and song—an island of tranquility in a sea of unrest—was difficult to fathom. We had had no idea what to expect.

The hours passed as though they were minutes. We became so engrossed in what was happening that we did not realize it was time to leave. The supervisors requested that we bid the inmates farewell and begin the exiting process.

As I was preparing to leave the room, a gentle-looking inmate of medium height, with short blond hair, rushed over to me with tears in his sad eyes. He had a modest and refined demeanor. He certainly did not look like the kind of guy you would find in a prison. Unfortunately, there are some Jews from religious backgrounds serving time in prison. In addition, there are other Jews who have discovered Yiddishkeit while in prison. These inmates are extremely committed. They pray together with a *minyan*, celebrate Shabbos and Yom Tov together, are meticulous about all religious observances and even organize Torah classes throughout the week. Kosher food is available, and some facilities even offer kosher food in their vending machines.

"My name is Meir ben Chana," he said. "I am facing fifteen years in this place. I wanted to know whether you would daven for me." He then lowered his eyes. I knew that, at that moment, he really needed some inspiring words. Suddenly a thought came to mind. I told him that according to the Chassidic Rebbes, if you think positively, it will be good. Something about those words penetrated his heart. He looked up at me, deep in concentration, and his entire face broke into a smile. I wished him well, promised to *daven* for him and promptly exited. For weeks, the prison scene re-played before my eyes, and Meir ben Chana, particularly, came to mind.

Three months later, a taxi driver knocked at the door of my home and brought the following message: "Meir ben Chana thanks you with all his heart and soul. Under a new government program, offenders who have committed a certain category of crime were released! Meir ben Chana belonged to this category and he was released as well."

It is an immense *mitzvah* to reach out to inmates and help them in any way that we can. The Rambam (Maimonides) elaborates on the law that *pidyon shevuyim* (redeeming captives) has top priority in terms of one's charity money. There are people in prison, who have not committed a crime deserving to serve time, but were simply given a harsh sentence. Others have committed much more serious crimes and get off without serving any time whatsoever in prison. However, it is the Torah outlook that no matter what a person has done, it is always possible for them to do *teshuva* and repent. It is especially during times when a person is in need that they need to know that their community has not abandoned them.

Once, while I was visiting a correctional facility, an officer remarked to me how inspiring it was for him to see that the Jewish people took such an interest in their brothers. They see to their needs, visit regularly, and continually remind them that they have not been forgotten. The officer said, "I only wish that was the case with the others."

One must always remember two statements of our Sages found in *Pirkei Avos*: "Do not judge your friend until you have reached his place" (2:4) and "Judge all men favorably" (1:6).

# WRONG TURN

*"And Hashem said to Moshe 'come to Pharaoh...'"
(Shemos 10:1). The great chassidic master Rabbi
Menachem Mendel of Kotzk asked a question.
Why does it say 'come to Pharaoh'? It should have
said 'go to Pharaoh'. The Kotzker explains that
the reason this language is used is because one
cannot go away from Hashem, for he is everywhere,
even in places seemingly devoid of holiness.*

# WRONG
# TURN

With the age of juvenile offenders getting younger every day, it is no longer a shock to hear about a teenager involved in a crime. However, even with an under-standing of the current situation concerning youth at risk in many of the Jewish communities, I must say that I was stunned by a call from desperate parents. They told me that their fourteen-year-old son, Shlomie*, was caught committing a federal crime and was being held in a locked facility. The parents said that their child had been troubled for as long as they could remember. He had not com-mitted this crime intentionally and certainly had no idea of the ram-ifications of his deed. The parents begged me to visit the young man and offer him some guidance and encouragement. Later that day, they arranged for a driver to take me on the two-and-a-half hour journey to the prison.

When I arrived, I was questioned, searched and led through a

* The names in the story have been changed to protect the identities of people involved.

number of electronic doors and gates until finally I reached a small room where I would be able to meet with this young man. Before Shlomie entered the room I wondered to myself what he would look like? A convict? A hoodlum? A gang member? All of a sudden the door opened and in walked a guard escorting a gentle looking, husky boy who walked slowly, his eyes lowered to the ground. You could tell that he had been through what no child should ever have to think about. He was embarrassed, ashamed and anguished by his plight. The guard left us sitting together at the table. I spoke to Shlomie, trying my best to be encouraging, recounting personal stories and anecdotes—anything to try and get through to him. Shlomie kept his eyes lowered and never once looked up. Occasionally, he answered a question with a barely audible yes or no. In the middle of our meeting, I learned that he was unable to obtain any type of snack at the facility, so I offered him a package of cookies and some fruit that I had brought with me. I asked him if he would like to have some. He answered affirmatively. When I put the food in front of him, he froze and sat completely still. I asked him if anything was wrong. Finally he looked up at me and said, "I would like to eat this, but I don't have a yarmulke." You could see that he was holding back his tears. I gave him my yarmulke and was overjoyed that at least I could do a little something for him. We had a long discussion and promised each other that we would keep in touch.

As they led Shlomie away, I thought to myself: convict? hoodlum? gang member? Hardly. Just one of Hashem's children who lost his way.

Too often we demonize and judge kids, or even adults, who have taken a wrong path. Many times these children's needs have not been met. Our system is not geared for those who may not meet our expectations.

Rabbi Chaim Sonnenfeld has said that every child should be treated as a potential *Moshiach*. He noted the verse in *Divrei Hayomim*, "Don't touch my annointed ones," to mean, "Do not, in any way, cause distress to the children." If we could instead open our hearts to children, listen to their conflicts and feel their pain and struggle, we could make *Klal Yisroel* as a whole that much stronger.

New York

# CALLER I.D.

*"Hakol b'yedei shomayim—Everything that happens has been Divinely pre-destined."*

# CALLER I.D.

On one of my many trips during the last four years to visit inmates of a New York penitentiary during the Yom Tov season I had the opportunity to say *Divrei Torah*. I was accompanied by various community activists. In addition, arrangements were made for the prisoners to hear some live Jewish music. As the music was playing, suddenly one of the inmates—a refined gentle soul, clearly a man from the religious community—took the microphone and began singing in accompaniment to a lively Hebrew song. All of the inmates were especially gratified to see an inmate performing and singing. Many of the inmates in the room were from a religious background and knew the words, so they began to join in. With each stanza, the singing grew stronger and more spiritual. Even some non-Jews who were not singing were caught up in the spiritual enthusiasm and clapped along. Before leaving, I chatted with a young man for about fifteen minutes about the challenges of prison life and what he wanted to do when he got out of prison.

Late that evening, after I arrived home, I received a telephone call from a woman who wanted to ask a question about an important matter in Jewish law. I discussed the issue with her. Before she hung up, she asked if she could call back in the future and immediately told me her name. When I heard the name, I realized that it was the same last name as the inmate who had been singing and dancing for everyone that afternoon. I was sure there could be no connection, but something inside me said, perhaps there was. I asked her if, by any chance, she could tell me her husband's first name. She did. I asked how her husband was doing, and she told me, "Honestly, right now he is serving time in prison."

At that moment I told her that I had, in fact, met her husband that day. I recounted how he had sung and danced, and how inspiring his performance had been for all the inmates.

She was clearly stunned and burst out crying. She explained in a choked voice that she had not heard from her husband recently and was depressed about this, worrying how well he was surviving life in prison. When she heard my report, it gave her new hope.

As I ended the conversation, I marveled at Divine Providence. Of all the rabbis in New York, she chose to call me on the day that I had the answer she needed most.

# THE
# FUTURE

# Serbia

# THE DANUBE—
# RIVER OF HOPE

*"Gazelles are the animals most loved
by G-d because a gazelle harms
no one and never disturbs the peace."*

—Midrash Shmuel *9*

### December 1999, Serbia and Montenegro

*U.S. Department of State Consular Information Sheet*

*Areas of Instability in Serbia: The potential for violent incidents persists throughout the country. Ethnic tensions remain high, particularly in the Kosovo and Sandzak regions. Travelers may be stopped by government militia at any time and should be prepared to cooperate. Border regions, particularly near Croatia and along the Drina River, are sensitive areas. There is a continuing trend toward lawlessness and disorder. Robberies are often perpetrated near railroad and bus stations, on public transport, and in city centers. Violent crime has increased dramatically, with many incidents taking place in broad daylight at popular public places. Possession of firearms (including grenades and mines) is widespread and weapons are frequently discharged in public.*

*There have been daily demonstrations in Belgrade and other urban centers since the municipal elections in Serbia. Clashes between demonstrators and police have occasionally resulted in severe injuries. American citizens are urged to exercise caution around all such demonstrations and rallies.*

### Bosnia and Herzegovina—Travel Warning

*The Department of State warns U.S. citizens not to travel to Bosnia and Herzegovina. Land mines and unexploded ordnance were left behind throughout the country after the war; roads, airports and railways have been bombed and are not functional. Sniping and car jacking are not uncommon. Law enforcement and civil authority have not been established in many regions. The December Dayton Peace Accords are being implemented with the NATO-led Implementation Force (IFOR) overseeing its military provisions. While progress in establishing a durable peace continues, the situation remains volatile. Medical Facilities: Health facilities are minimal or non-existent; most medicines are not obtainable.*

# THE DANUBE—
# RIVER OF HOPE

Usually when one has a fear of flying, it is a fear of losing control, of being up in the air without an anchor. There are even schools offering classes that help to alleviate these fears and gradually train a person to tolerate airplane flight.

Traveling over the Balkans on a bitter cold Tuesday morning, I experienced not a fear of flying, but rather a fear of landing. While planning this trip, my associate, Eliezer Allman, and I had received several written warnings concerning the danger and inadvisability of taking such a trip. Although thousands of international peace-keepers had been deployed in Bosnia to keep a sort of nascent peace, billions of dollars in international assistance would be needed to repair the massive destruction that had taken place in the country over which I was now hovering. The horrific toll is beyond imagination; 250,000 dead, 200,000 wounded and more than two million refugees. A third of all the roads and forty percent of the country's bridges were destroyed.

It has been said by political analysts that, "This was the war of fear, a war of the mind—a hate that has destroyed a country and divided its people." The Jewish community of Belgrade had asked me to come to give seminars about Yiddishkeit and the nature of belief. It was to these people that I hoped to be able to provide *chizuk* (encouragement) and inspiration. The Rabbi of the Jewish community wanted to give the Jewish community—particularly the young people—more exposure to Judaism. The war had added urgency to this Rabbi's quest. As our *Chachomim* (Sages) have said, "A little bit of light dispels much darkness" (Rabbi Yisroel Salanter).

As our Czech-Air flight touched down at Belgrade, there was no customary round of applause from the passengers. All nine of our fellow passengers quietly disembarked from the plane. The Belgrade airport was low-key. As we grabbed our baggage from the conveyor belt and headed toward customs, we were met by an unusually gifted young man, Mark. Mark was an upper classman, a student at the local university. I use the word "student" advisedly because there had been no classes for the past year due to the closings of all schools from nursery through university. I had the opportunity to visit the local university during my stay. Walking down the halls, there was an eerie silence. The voice of education had been stilled and thousands of students had little to do during the day. Some of the students now spent their time participating in the daily massive public demonstrations during which hundreds of thousands of people banded together in solidarity.

Mark, with his sterling personality and eloquence, began to explain his country's recent history and some of the problems it currently faced. As we passed the signs for Zagreb and Sarajevo, my mind and heart tried to fathom the depths of what had transpired on the land on which we were traveling. Throughout my stay, as I visited with individuals and groups, I was to witness firsthand the devastating effects of war. The poor economic condition, lack of provisions and the scarcity of water and telephone were but a few examples.

War had cast its shadow and it would be some time before the sun's radiance would penetrate the horizon. I was also given a thorough tour of the country, the schools, the shops, the archives, neighborhoods both urban and rural, the *shuls* and the cemeteries.

Our schedule was action-packed, during which time I met some fascinating personalities. I had the privilege of meeting with the Minister of Religion, Minister Dragolovich. In the course of this most meaningful visit, Minister Dragolovich expressed his particular appreciation for the

*Rabbi Goldwasser with Minister Dragolovich.*

opportunity to share his feelings and concerns about the present situation of his country. As we embraced, before I took my leave, we promised to continue a joint effort on behalf of peace and freedom. Minister Dragolovich's refined character and patient demeanor have contributed to the effective use of his good offices for the cause of humanity. I will never forget our inspirational meeting.

It was on the last night of our stay in Serbia that I had the privilege of meeting with a large group at the Jewish community center. After the years of war, the current unrest and the resultant precarious situation that these people now faced, everyone needed inspiration. I hoped to be a source of that inspiration and encourage these people to face the challenges of the future.

It was a bitter cold night, but the atmosphere in the community center situated on the third floor above the synagogue was aglow. The room—no larger than a small classroom—was crammed with people. In fact, whenever someone new arrived, it was difficult to enter through the single door. The dim lighting contributed to the mystique of the evening. For three and a half hours I spoke, lectured, related moving incidents, and answered questions posed to me. The atmosphere was super-charged. The group's palpable excited anticipation and absorption of every word was indescribable. By the end of the night we had discussed issues of heaven and earth, life and death, freedom and exile, G-d and man, war and peace. After wishing each other well and making arrangements to keep in touch, we said goodbye as most of the group faded into the night.

As we walked back with our guide through the alleyway to the street where our hotel was located, a young lady who had participated in the evening's event approached me and, with a sense of urgency in her voice, inquired whether she could ask me a question. I naturally responded in the affirmative. She began: "Allow me to introduce myself. I am from Sarajevo. I was born and raised there. I had a happy childhood. Right before the war began, I was seriously thinking of marriage. However, as my life was torn asunder, so were my plans. After experiencing the darkness and the horrors of the war years, depression crept in and I became distraught. I no longer wished to get married and I gave up my dream of having a child. I would never want to bring a child into such a world! How could I, ever?" As she ended her emotional statement, I realized that although the clouds of despair and disillusionment hovered over her, she was still searching for validation.

I answered by relating an incident that had taken place in Eastern Europe after a pogrom had destroyed the city's main synagogue. An old man began to sift through the rubble of the destroyed remains. He found a brick that was still whole. He scurried to a corner and stored the brick. He returned to the ruins, found a piece of wood that had not been burnt and stored it together with the brick. As he continued to accumulate a pile of remnants, onlookers gathered. One arrogant observer said mockingly to the old man, "You old fool, what are you doing? Everything has been destroyed." The old man looked up and, with conviction in his eyes, answered, "It is precisely now that I am rebuilding for the future." I continued, "You, who have harmed no one, must not despair any longer. If you do you will only be hurting yourself. Pick up the remnants of your life and build anew, and G-d will surely help."

As I have witnessed so many times through the end of the war, people needed to find reasons to hope for a better future. Many, like

*Some Jews in Serbia with Rabbi Goldwasser (second from left).*

this woman, still had that hope, but they needed encouragement to go on.

In the Torah (*Bamidbar [Numbers]* 23:24) it says, "*Heyn am kalavi yakum uch'ari yisnaseh*—they are a nation that will arise like a lion cub and raise itself like a lion." Even after experiencing destruction and devastation, the people of Israel have the amazing power of resilience to restore their life to its former glory.

# Bosnia

# CHILDREN OF
# THE WAR

*"What was their crime? Only that they were born."*

—*Chassidic saying*

# CHILDREN
# OF THE WAR

I had traveled through Bosnia at the behest of the local Jewish community. I was asked to check on what remained of the Jewish cemetery. They wanted me to survey the cemetery and make recommendations on repairs according to Jewish law. A philanthropist had provided a driver and a luxury Mercedes car, the likes of which most local people had never seen.

As we were traveling back from the cemetery, the sun was setting. We found ourselves in a narrow alley, halted behind a stopped army supply truck. It was impossible to pass, and we were forced to wait until the truck moved. As we sat there, we could see people in the town stopping to stare at our clearly expensive car. Nearly all the cars on the road were ten—even twenty—years old and here we were in a luxurious imported car.

At that moment I heard a knock at my window. I turned and saw two children—one probably six or seven years old; the other looked like he was barely three or four. The children begged me to open the window. The driver told me in English, "Don't even think about opening it. There are thousands of beggars. Open the window and you'll invite more trouble than we need."

I glanced back at the two young children and saw the desperation in their eyes. It was impossible for me not to be moved. I decided that, regardless of the risk involved, my heart would not allow me to ignore their pleas.

As I rolled down the window just a few inches, I put out my hand and extended my arm downward to give them a dollar bill. The older one immediately grabbed the dollar and put it inside his shirt.

With that, the younger one brought his head back, opened his mouth and pointed to the inside of his mouth, clearly trying to tell me that he was starving.

I found a pre-packaged container of applesauce which I began to lower down to him from the window. However, before it reached his little hands, the quick-thinking older boy grabbed the package away and ran off into the sunset.

At that point, the little boy began to cry—not tears that you and I are used to, but tears that came jumping out of his eyes in a bitter awful wail.

I frantically searched inside the car until I found a snack that I knew he would like. I put my arm out again with the snack in hand and lowered it until it reached his little hands. He took my hand, kissed and hugged it.

That child's face will forever remain etched in my soul.

♦ ♦ ♦ ♦

It is quite difficult to put into words the devastation that I witnessed in Bosnia. Walking through the streets and seeing rows of houses completely leveled, and bombed-out buildings, libraries, hospitals, and schools had a great impact. Seeing starving people who had nothing to eat, whose homes had been destroyed, and whose prospects for the future were at best dismal, compels one to do some deeper thinking. Observing the horrendous aftermath of a war forces one to confront issues of life and death and man's purpose in this world.

I personally was moved to *teshuva*, to introspection. Our Chazal tell us that when we see the Divine attribute of strict justice manifest itself in the world—when something bad happens anywhere—it is a message to us throughout the world to fix our deeds, to improve our lives, and to come closer to Hashem.

I also accepted upon myself not to take for granted the small things in life that we expect to happen just as a matter of nature.

# Bosnia

# ARTICLE OF FAITH

*"It is a well known law that Eisav hates Yaakov."*

—Bereishis, Rashi *33:4*

*The brilliant scientist Albert Einstein attended many scientific conferences. At one conference of highly accomplished scientists, there was a particular scientist known to be a rabid anti-Semite. Before the proceedings of the conference began, the anti-Semitic professor shouted to Einstein so that all could hear, "Einstein, Einstein, don't you wish that you wouldn't have been born a Jew?" Einstein paused momentarily and then said, "Yes, I do. Because then I could have become a Jew on my own!"*

*Anti-Semitism, like any baseless hate, is a problem that has spanned the millennia. In the Torah, we read of Kain who could not tolerate his brother Hevel; Eisav who hated Yaakov; Pharaoh who despised Moshe; and so it has continued for thousands of years. Intolerance, prejudice and persecution have found expression in the most civilized of nations, the most cultured of men and women. Yet, as researchers continue to grapple with the causes of enmity in the world, it seems as though there is no answer, rhyme or reason for why people hate.*

# ARTICLE
# OF FAITH

I t was a sunny, yet cold day in March as I found myself sitting amongst thirty assorted passengers—all locals—on a bus traveling from one part of Bosnia to another, crossing the demilitarized zone in-between.

The five-hour bus ride was for the most part uneventful. However, as the bus approached the border, things suddenly changed. From each of the military groups stationed at the border, soldiers came and boarded the bus. These soldiers requested visas and passports from each passenger. The first group of soldiers boarded the bus without much fanfare. Suddenly, the atmosphere intensified as the last officer began his investigation. No longer did people engage in any conversation. Everyone sat quietly at attention—nobody moved. The air felt heavy with fear and tension. This officer's posture also differed from the others. He commanded—no, he demanded—absolute respect and obedience. In contrast to the others, his questions were lengthy and often obtrusive. One could sense

*Checkpoint in Bosnia.*

a feeling of nervous panic as the officer stood before each passenger.

I was seated in the back row of the bus, the last available seat. Soon it was my turn to be questioned. Although at times it was suggested that I wear casual clothing to camouflage my faith whenever I travel, I have always ascribed to the philosophy of truth that, "we are what we are." As the old adage goes, "The best lie is the truth." As soon as the officer noticed me, he singled me out and told me to stand. I wondered why I was being treated differently than the others. He asked for my passport and appropriate papers and then began to stare at the top of my head. He asked me a question in his native tongue, a language I do not understand. Not receiving a response, he motioned with both of his hands, pointing to the top of my head. Becoming agitated, he repeated his question over and over again, as if his repetition would jar me into comprehension. Finally, I realized that he must be asking me about the *yarmulka* that I always wear on the top of my head. I tried to explain, "It's a *yarmulka*." His facial expression became contorted, which conveyed to me that he still did not understand and was growing impatient for a satisfactory explanation. I continued to try to offer other explanations, none of which he could understand. By this time all the other passengers on the bus turned and began staring at me. The officer turned to the passengers and said something to them that caused them to laugh. I later found out that he had indeed made a snide remark about me. Finally, one of the passengers who knew how to speak English, helped the officer. I was then asked in a derogatory manner, "Is that your religion?" I looked him straight in the eye and answered, "No, it is my life." I would not be intimidated. The sole purpose of wearing a *yarmulka* is to remind us of the One Above and to instill in us a fear of G-d.

Through the ages Jews have been challenged to stand up and confront provocation. It really isn't that difficult if you remember that there is G-d above and He alone is Whom we must revere. "Officers have pursued me without cause, but it is the word of G-d that my heart fears" (*Psalms* 119:161).

# NO MAN'S LAND

*When Yocheved placed Moshe into the Nile,
she also made him a* chupah *(wedding canopy)
which she placed in his basket. We learn from
this how important it is to have faith, even in
the most trying of times. Can you possibly
imagine a more devastating moment for a
mother than when she is forced to place her
own child in a basket into the water because
she fears he will be drowned by the king's
soldiers? Despite everything, Yocheved did
not lose hope, but with confidence she built
a* chupah *for her child. Her hope turned out
not to be in vain."*

—Midrash Shemos *1:28*

*It has been said that the Republic of Bosnia, Herzegovina, is like a trauma patient kept alive through heroic measures and invasive technology. Over 60,000 NATO-led peace-keeping troops have been dispatched to separate the combatants, in order to allow every area to have a chance to recover from the worst atrocities and destruction in Europe since World War II. Yugoslavia has been termed a house much divided. Sarajevo was a sitting duck for enemy fire. Bosnia's capital could be seen from a vantage point above the Romanija Mountains. From there, Serb artillery relentlessly pounded the city for most of the war. Gunfire from surrounding neighborhoods south of the Miljacka River claimed even more victims during the siege, which had begun when snipers fired into a crowd of demonstrators rallying for a free Bosnia.*

*Sarajevo, once a cosmopolitan city of beautiful, lush hills that had hosted the World Olympics, is now in a state of destruction. Sixty percent of the houses in Bosnia, half the schools, and a third of the hospitals were razed or damaged. Power plants, roads, and water systems lie in ruins. Fields and vineyards were abandoned and rivers contaminated by toxic waste. The soil is polluted with millions of earth-shattering land mines. Billions of dollars and billions of prayers will be needed in the years ahead to mend and repair, both physically and psychologically, this shattered land.*

# NO MAN'S
# LAND

I had received a plea to travel to Croatia and Bosnia and spend
Shabbos with a group of people who had an urgent thirst for
spirituality. They not only hadn't had a rabbi since the 1940's,
but they had just gone through a horrifying war. Realizing the
urgency of the request and what it would mean to people living
through such troubled times, I couldn't refuse. And so I was booked
on a connecting flight Thursday evening leaving New York's J.F.K.
Airport for Vienna and continuing on to Bosnia with my final destination—Sarajevo. The flight Thursday evening was delayed for one
hour in the airport and one hour on the runway. My connecting
flight in Vienna was scheduled to leave within forty-five minutes of
my arrival. I asked the flight personnel what they thought my
chances were of my making the connecting flight. They assured me
that there would be no problem. However, even with their assurance, I can't say that I wasn't concerned. Sure enough, moments
after the flight landed in Vienna Friday morning, as I rushed to the

connecting flight, I was informed that the flight had just left. I raced to the transfer desk and was told that it would be impossible to make a connection that would arrive in time for Shabbos. In fact, there would be no flights connecting to Sarajevo until possibly Sunday evening. I couldn't believe it! I had traveled to Europe, blocked out my entire schedule in order to spend Shabbos with these people, and now I was faced with the possibility that the trip might have been in vain!

I explained to the airline supervisor how important it was that I get to Sarajevo in time for Shabbos. I was almost in tears and I begged for understanding. When the supervisor realized the urgency of this mission she told me to wait a moment and went into a back office. Moments later she emerged, smiling. "We have arranged for a jet to fly you to your destination." Airline personnel soon arrived to escort me to the plane. To my surprise, I was the only passenger in a small plane.

The far-reaching hand of *hashgacha pratis* (Divine Providence) moved swiftly that Friday afternoon and, miraculously, I arrived in time for Shabbos. I was told that usually fifteen to twenty people show up for the Friday night services. However, some additional preparations were made due to the fact that word had spread about the special guest the community would be hosting that Shabbos. The beautiful shul that once stood so proudly in the center of town had been destroyed—it had actually been systematically bombed in sections. Today, the only indication that a shul once stood there is a plaque on a brick wall of a parking lot. The group was to meet in the synagogue which is currently housed in the community center. Incidentally, this center was also recently bombed and newly rebuilt. The hints of war and unrest were certainly there. As I entered through the outside doors of the community center, I noticed a special electronic door with lights and detectors that everyone had to pass through. It was a special security measure that had now become a way of life. By way of a glass window inside the entrance, a guard monitored each person who entered.

As I made my way through security I saw dear friends who were waiting for my arrival. They were immensely excited and eagerly anticipated experiencing the Shabbos that their *neshomos* (souls) yearned for. One of the people said, "You

*Arrival in Sarajevo. Inset: Sarajevo International Airport.*

won't believe it, but we've never had this many people here." Hundreds had crowded into the community center's allotted space for the *shul*. That evening we *davened* (prayed) and sang together. In fact, the *tefillos* (prayers) took on an added dimension because of the life and death situation that the people of this land had faced.

An elderly woman approached me and asked if I would say the Kaddish for her husband. She explained that her husband had died during the war and throughout these difficult years she had never found someone to say Kaddish for his soul. She said that tonight would be his *yahrtzeit* (the anniversary date of a person's passing). I told her at once that it would be my privilege to say Kaddish for her husband.

Following the prayers, we all assembled in a large room where I recited the Kiddush for everyone. I personally poured a little bit of wine from the cup for each person. The spirit in the room that

*Synagogue in Sarajevo.*

evening was contagious. We sang, we learned, we ate, and we discussed various topics of Torah, continuing late into the night. One of the middle-aged men came to me with his cup of wine and asked me whether he had to drink it, or if he could save it for a future happy occasion (since kosher wine was difficult to obtain). I told him he could drink some of it and save the rest. I returned to my room early in the morning exhausted, yet exhilarated from one of the most special Friday nights that I had ever experienced.

The next day we studied and *davened* together throughout the day. The same elderly woman approached me, and fully repeated her request that I say Kaddish for her husband at Shacharis. She then came to me once again before Mincha—I assured her that I would recite the Kaddish. We said farewell to the Shabbos with a Torah class that lasted from 4:00 p.m. until 10:00 p.m. After the class, I continued to answer personal questions from various individuals. Then I noticed the elderly woman waiting to speak to me. She said to me, "Because you redeemed my husband's soul after all these years, I would like to redeem the Kaddish that you said." She told me her name was Leah* and she presented me with what looked like a round object wrapped in silver foil. She explained that the coin was over one hundred years old and was the last possession that she had of her husband's. She wanted me to have it. I politely refused by saying that it is important for her to have a memento. She then said, "Up until now the coin was my memento, but from this day onwards, I no longer need the coin for I have the Kaddish."

The next morning at 8:00 a.m. I was preparing to leave for the airport to fly into Sarajevo. Before I left, I wanted to say goodbye to the elderly woman who had asked me to say Kaddish. I got her telephone number from the community center and when I dialed her number a young person answered. When I asked to speak with Leah, the young person said, "I'm so sorry. Leah passed on early this morning." I then learned that her husband hadn't died in the recent civil strife, but during World War II. For one reason or another, she had been unable to find anyone to say Kaddish for him. She willed herself to stay alive for another fifty years until she could perform this final duty.

The first thing that I saw when I landed in Sarajevo was a soldier in battle array, with his machine gun drawn, waiting and observing as each individual deplaned. The airport was "no frills." The interior could be compared to a darkened warehouse. There

* The names in the story have been changed to protect the identities of people involved.

*Bombed out building in Sarajevo.*

was a customs officer in a small booth who carefully looked over each person's papers. When it was my turn, he looked through my passport, noting the visas that I had for Serbia. The Serbs and the people of Sarajevo were on opposing sides during the war; one can imagine that there was not much goodwill generated by the horrific war that took place there. I explained that at the time I could only fly into Serbia. My explanation was accepted and soon I was riding in a small taxi to my quarters in Sarajevo.

The echoes of the war could be heard throughout the land. It was overwhelming to view the destruction that had taken place. Building after building was bombed. Some leveled to the ground. Skyscrapers completely blown apart. Houses ripped in half. The first sign one sees while traveling from the airport is one that had been written in large letters. It says it all so succinctly: "WELCOME TO THE WAR."

*Scene of destruction in Sarajevo.*

I traveled to the place where I was to stay—a hotel now taken over by the military. And, since the community center was not open yet, I decided to visit the local cemetery, as is my custom when I travel. After a half hour walk, my guide and I reached the cemetery atop a winding road. The cemetery was the dividing line in the war between the Serbs and the opposing army. It has been said that the most ferociously contested four acres in Bosnia was this cemetery. The first thing that we noticed was a large trench that surrounded the inside wall of the cemetery. On the cemetery gates a sign was posted, "Forbidden to Enter. Danger." We discussed whether this sign was still in force or whether it had been especially constructed for the war. As I was climbing through the foxhole an older woman began yelling from the road. "No! No! Don't go there. No!" She hurried to tell us that just a week ago some dogs had gone into the cemetery and were blown apart when they stepped on land mines! She offered to show us the small area at the entrance where we could safely walk.

A magnificent chapel is located inside the cemetery near the entrance. The chapel, painted beautifully, had a Turkish look to it, with huge round domes. However, the war had taken its toll. A huge chunk of the dome had been bombed and the special writing on the dome was no longer discernible. Inside the chapel, all had been cleared out. There were only piles upon piles

*Chapel of the cemetery destroyed by bombs.*

of sand bags, indicating that the soldiers had used the chapel as a fort. It was sad to think about all the fighting, bombing and shooting that had taken place in the cemetery. After all, in the *Yizkor* (memorial prayer), we daven that those who pass on should rest peacefully in their place. What kind of peace did the *neshomos* (souls) in that cemetery have?

After saying a brief *tefillah* (prayer), we walked back to the center of town. To be sure, I was extremely careful with my every step. In the middle of the sidewalk, every so often, I would see a gaping hole where the cement had cracked and caved in. In the center of the hole one could see an exploded grenade, untouched. I guess I was not used to seeing so much destruction up close. Soldiers swarmed through the streets. We walked past the central library. It was completely destroyed. All two million precious volumes and documents had been blown to smithereens in seconds. All of this was getting to me. It was a heady experience that deeply touched me. At night, my head was heavy with the memories of everything I had seen. I then

*Aftermath of war in Sarajevo.*

made the mistake of looking out of the window of my room. Across the street was a building, completely bombed out. Needless to say, it was impossible to fall asleep.

I was looking for some inspiration, for some measure of solace that would help to place all that I had witnessed into perspective. We reached the community center and met with some members who had come to this active center that served as a meeting place, synagogue, soup kitchen, place of public assistance and nerve center. After talking for a while, a man and a woman appeared and introduced themselves as the teachers of a group of children who were meeting at that very moment on the fourth floor of the community center. The woman said, "I know you are busy and probably don't have the time, but I wanted to invite you to see the children of Sarajevo in their class." At once I told the teacher it would be my privilege to meet the children. I then proceeded up the steep flight of stairs to the room that served as the school. As the door opened, I instantly received the inspiration that I so desperately needed. There, inside the room, were children of all ages, seated quietly around the table, playing games and quietly talking with their friends. I was asked if I would like to speak to the children, but I opted to get to know them first. These children had lived through a horrific war. They fell asleep in their little beds to the sound of bombs and were exposed to horrors that most of us will hopefully never see in a lifetime.

However, even during the darkest hours of the war, these children continued to attend this Jewish school. Each week they came to be identified with the Jewish community and lay claim to their precious heritage. The teacher's personal *mesiras nefesh* (self-sacrifice) was to provide the children with some semblance of normalcy. I took a seat around the low table, with the children circled all around me. I began to play one of the small games that was on the table with some of the children. The children were quite excited by my participation and tried to express themselves. After about fifteen minutes of playing, I happened to notice the teacher who had invited me. She had tears streaming down her cheeks. I guess for

*A Jewish school in Sarajevo (Rabbi Goldwasser, right).*

her it was overwhelming. A Rabbi had come from afar to visit these precious children, survivors of the war, and they were actually playing a game. I felt that in this particular situation my participation in their moments of relaxation and fun would be far more effective than any speech. I handed out candies to the children and spoke briefly with each of them.

It was difficult for me to leave the classroom. I felt that I needed to do more to erase their pain and give them back the childhood that had been taken from them. Tears were now in my eyes as I was presented with a scroll of artwork by the children of Sarajevo. It is something that I shall forever cherish.

*Mincha in Serbia.*

*Rabbi Goldwasser (right) with former Chief Rabbi Tzaddik Danon.*

# Skopje, Macedonia

# TIME TO COME HOME

*"... and there is nothing left but this Torah."*

—*Yom Kippur Services, Ne'ilah*

On Chanukah we celebrate the victory of the Chashmonaim *over the* Yevonim *(Hellenists), in which the small Maccabean army was able to overtake the massive and powerful Greek army. We also celebrate the following miracle. When the Jews entered the defiled and desecrated Holy Temple, they wanted to light the* menorah *(a candelabra which was to be kept lit each day). They found only one cruse of oil with the seal of the* Kohen Gadol *(High Priest) still intact. Ordinarily, the oil in that cruse would only be enough to last one day. It would take eight days to produce new oil suitable for the* menorah. *A miracle occurred, and the small cruse of oil that was only supposed to last one day kept the* menorah *lit for eight days. To commemorate this miracle, we light the* menorah, *adding one additional candle each night for all the eight days of Chanukah.*

*Over the centuries, commentators have asked why Chanukah is celebrated for eight days. After all, the real miracle lasted only seven days, when the Jews discovered enough oil to burn for one night and the oil then lasted for eight days.*

*The renowned Chassidic master, Rabbi Menachem Mendel of Kotzk, had an interesting answer. He noted that the miracle of the first day was that after the Jews had experienced so much destruction and devastation, they even bothered to look for the oil at all.*

# TIME TO
# COME HOME

In the Talmud (*Bava Metziah*, 85a), it is written, *"Amar R' Yirmiyah, Torah machzeres al achsanya shela*—the Torah naturally returns to its home."* The great scholar, the Maharshah, explains that this means that if we exert effort, the Torah of our ancestors will assist us in reaching our level of learning.

Until recently, when I traveled to the city of Skopje, Macedonia, I never fully comprehended the meaning of this piece of Talmud. I was called upon to celebrate the opening of a shul for the first time in fifty-seven years—since the devastation of the *Shoah* (Holocaust).

Arrangements for the trip were made by R' Eliezer Allman and Mrs. Sonya Samokovlija. They had asked me to fly from Zurich to Skopje, Macedonia, to give *chizuk* to the local people. Macedonia is located at the southern end of the former Yugoslavia, approximately twenty kilometers from the border of Kosovo. Its Jewish heritage dates back to the Roman times. Before the Second World War, 8,000 Jews lived in Macedonia. During the Second World War, they lived under Bulgarian occupation. Then the majority of the Jewish population was deported to their deaths. Only ten percent of the Macedonian community survived. The remaining Jewish community is now based in the capital of Skopje. Until now, there had been no synagogues and the few Jews left had hardly any connection with formal Jewish life.

Aboard the plane to Skopje, I sat next to Dr. Azis Pollozhani. He turned out to be a high-ranking member of Parliament/Assembly of the Republic of Macedonia. He briefed me on the current state of affairs in Macedonia and the challenges his country faces. He graciously welcomed me to the country and pledged to use his good offices to assist our efforts in any way possible. Dr. Pollozhani's warm reception helped to ease whatever fears I had as I entered this unfamiliar land.

As we disembarked and entered the small airport in Skopje, it was immediately discernible that this was not a modern city. It was as though one had entered a time warp into a land that had resisted or wasn't even aware of the advances of modern technology. The small airport offered few services. I had wanted to make a telephone call; however, this was a feat I would have no success accomplishing.

The organizer of my trip, Mrs. Sonya Samokovlija, met me at the plane with a car and driver. She guided the driver to the Jewish Community Center. Along the way I was deeply affected by some of the scenes of poverty we encountered in the streets. Mountain goats, sheep and rams roamed freely. A truck that looked like a relic from the war more than fifty years ago could not make it up a small hill, and a dozen or so local people from the village helped to push the truck. A tow truck seemed a still undiscovered innovation.

As we passed through the center of the city, we saw evidence of the devastating earthquake that had taken place in Macedonia. The clock in the watchtower stopped at the moment of the earthquake and had never moved forward, similar to certain aspects of Macedonia.

As our car reached the Jewish Community Center, we were greeted by a few members of the Jewish Community, eagerly awaiting our arrival. They enthusiastically showed me the new shul. I was overwhelmed with emotion. The *bais medrash* had been built in magnificent taste, complete with stained glass windows and a display of antique Judaica.

Standing in the *bais medrash*, I was unexpectedly greeted by one of my dearest friends, the Chief Rabbi of Serbia, Rabbi Yitzchak Asiel and his Rebbetzin, Rachel. The meeting was emotional, for it had been more than two years since I had last seen Rabbi Asiel. Since the war had broken out in Serbia, I had to unfortunately interrupt my usual travel to Belgrade. Communication during those months was sometimes difficult, and even e-mails had been impossible. I shall never forget the letters the Rabbi and his wife had sent to me describing the *matzav ruach* (situation and atmosphere) of the community during the war. They had proved their selfless dedication and *mesiras nefesh* by standing by with their community during the entire war—exemplary role models for all to learn from.

As I spoke to Rabbi Asiel, I noticed the *paroches* (curtain) adorning the *aron hakodesh* looked as if it had been used in a different generation. The *paroches* was made of a worn maroon velvet with faded gold lettering. The words Skopje,

*Dedication of Torah in Macedonia.*

Macedonia, were written on it in Hebrew. There was something

familiar about it. I thought I had seen it somewhere before.

When I asked Rabbi Asiel about this, he remarked that I was right! I had seen the *paroches* on display with other relics of the past in an exhibit in Belgrade. It had been finally returned to Skopje for its proper use in the new shul.

I observed the brand new *siddurim* and *chumashim*, and the special pamphlets of explanation written in Macedonian that had been brought in for the occasion. The entire city was caught up in the excitement of the dedication. The non-Jewish Macedonian population had always had a good relationship with the Jewish people. Many dignitaries and representatives of other religious groups arrived to show their support and participate in a special dedication concert featuring the Macedonia Philharmonic Orchestra and Chazzan Joseph Malovany of New York.

Later that evening I met people who had come from many surrounding countries. They were caught up in the enthusiasm of this historic event—the first shul in Macedonia in fifty-seven years. I will never forget meeting one Jewish man living in Kosovo. He described to me his sincerity and commitment to maintain a strong tie to Yiddishkeit.

As we were about to leave, an amazing piece of information was revealed. Historic records showed that the last day that the Torah had been read in Macedonia was the day that the Nazis had marched on Skopje and deported the Jewish community. That day was the fourth of Adar II, 1943. Fifty-seven years later, the day of the dedication of the new shul, when the Torah once again would be unrolled to be read for the community, was none other than the fourth day of Adar II, 2000.

"*Torah machzeres al achsanya shela*—the Torah naturally returns to its home."

Monticello, New York

# YOURS, MINE OR OURS

*"We learn best what our heart prepares us to learn."*

—Talmud Avodah Zarah *19*

*In the* Book of Prophets, Isaiah *(54:13) it says, "And all your children should be learned in Hashem's ways."*

*Commentators on this verse ask: Why is it written, "all your children"? It could merely have said, "The children should be learned in Hashem's ways."*

*The Torah means to underscore that* all *children need to be taught, regardless of their strengths or weaknesses. Each child, no matter what challenges he or she may face in life, deserves the finest Torah education that the community can provide.*

*It says in* Psalms *(60:6): "Nosato li'yere'acha nes l'hisnosses —You have given a banner to those who fear You so that it should be displayed." The word "nes," besides meaning "banner," can also mean "test"—signifying that tests are the banners Hashem uses to display the high levels of those people. The challenge of educating every child is not limited to his or her parents. It is a challenge to the entire community. In recent years, we have begun to attempt to raise that banner.*

# YOURS, MINE
# OR OURS

A weekend convention in upstate New York was being planned. Hundreds of teenagers throughout North America were expected to attend. The intention of this gathering was to achieve an inspirational and exalted atmosphere— one that would create everlasting memories that could be evoked by the teenagers for years to come.

As the date neared, I received a phone call from an organization requesting that ten paraplegic teenagers be encouraged to participate in the weekend activities. Knowing that these special children would immeasurably add to the atmosphere, I promptly, without hesitation, agreed that they be included.

That evening, I summarized the conversation to the planning committee. Unfortunately, my suggestion was not met with the same enthusiasm that I felt for it; they brought up objections—"We don't have the proper facilities for these children," "It will be disruptive to the smooth flow of the convention program," and so on, as they expressed their criticism and displeasure. One member even blurted out, "I don't know how *our* children will react!" This comment, in particular, stabbed at me. Until this time, I hadn't seen differences. All of us are children of the same ancestors. I was astonished that anybody would make distinctions between children of varying gifts. After a somewhat tenuous discussion, I was able to convince the committee members that these children *did* belong at the event.

Finally the day of the event arrived. Throngs of teenagers gathered in the hotel lobby. They seemed to have come from all walks of life. Distinct traces of "Americana" could be heard. One needed only to pause and listen to the various inflections of speech to determine where in America each teenager resided.

A large van made its way to the entrance of the hotel. Suddenly, a group of wheelchair-bound teenagers made their way up the ramp to the doors, and into the hotel lobby. Their faces beamed with exuberance. You could tell how much they desired to be accepted and be part of this "normal" group of teens. In no time at all, their abundant enthusiasm ignited everyone and had a profound impact on each and every teenager. The adult leaders were also awed by these kids' zeal and eagerness.

At one point, several circles were formed and the young people began to sing and dance. The spiritual atmosphere was inspiring and contagious with euphoric and uplifting songs and lively dancing. All those present were visibly enchanted.

During the course of the festivities, it became an honor to escort the wheelchair-bound teens to join in the circles. All the teenagers made an extra effort to befriend the special kids, although this was easy, since they were all personable and their fervor was infectious.

Impulsively, I grabbed hold of a young boy named Mike* in a wheelchair and began to wheel him toward one of the circles. Suddenly, Mike, with his cherubic face, big brown eyes and curly brown hair, tugged at my sleeve. He gestured to me to crouch down so that he could whisper in my ear. His impish grin and shy demeanor piqued my curiosity. I bent down and he whispered intensely, "You know, I don't actually know the song, but I'm still singing!"

We all know the song, but how many of us are actually singing?

We shouldn't allow the opportunities to bring people together to pass us by. Sometimes people living with a challenge teach us so much about both life and about ourselves. People who face physical challenges expend tremendous effort to achieve; they yearn to use their abilities and their gifts as best they can. Their struggle should serve as a powerful lesson for all of us who are more privileged.

* The names in the story have been changed to protect the identities of people involved.

Elizabeth, New Jersey

# FOR THIS CHILD
# I PRAYED

*"For this child I prayed…"*

—Shmuel I *1:27*

*In repeated clinical trials it has been proven that the mind-body connection is so powerful that when patients are spoken to with hope, encouragement and optimism, their treatment and healing is enhanced.*

*In one anecdote revealing the mind-body connection, Dr. Lawrence Golding of the Royal Hospital in London reported the story of a person who came into the hospital for routine blood tests. Through a technical error, his physician informed him that he had been stricken with a terrible disease. The patient's health slowly began to deteriorate. Soon it was revealed that he was actually in perfect health and there had been an error. He had simply been an obedient patient—and even though there had been nothing wrong with him, his body had cooperated with the diagnosis and had begun to fail.*

*This anecdote has been replicated in different countries and situations. In each case, the patient's health declined following a negative diagnosis, even though in all these cases the diagnosis was in error.*

# FOR THIS
# CHILD I PRAYED

Expectant parents experience an exciting and joyful time of anticipation. There are so many preparations, visits to the doctor's office, browsing through department stores for baby furniture, and attending Lamaze classes. In addition to the physical preparations, expectant parents must also be emotionally prepared to become parents. This means knowing that when the happy day arrives, their lives will radically change and be immeasurably enriched.

One particular young couple, Ira and Alysia Heller, looked forward with eager anticipation to the happy event and prayed to be blessed with a healthy baby. As Alysia entered her eighth month, she and Ira went to the hospital for a routine sonogram. The sonographer detected a problem in the fetus's development. The doctor verified the situation—it was serious. Specialists in neonatalogy were immediately consulted. The conferring physicians concurred that the baby would definitely be neurologically impaired. The couple anxiously inquired whether there was any chance that there may be room for error. The doctor's reply was a firm "No."

Ira and Alysia firmly resolved that regardless of what the doctors declared, the *Ribono Shel Olam* (Master of the World) is the One who is in charge of life in this world. They therefore decided not to put their faith in the doctors' predictions.

During the following month, each day seemed endless. They shared the immense excitement and anticipation that all expectant parents experience; but, these feelings were tempered with trepidation as well as fear of the unknown. *Tefillos* (prayers) were said throughout the world on behalf of their unborn baby.

Alysia delivered a beautiful baby girl. Emotions in the delivery room ran the complete gamut, as Tehila emerged into this world. There was a radiance, an aura which filled the entire room. The doctors were well prepared. The group of neonatalogists were at the ready. The baby was wrapped up and prepared for her transfer to the neonatal intensive care unit. Alysia was deprived of the opportunity that every mother longs for—to hold her baby close to her immediately after the birth. However, Alysia held on to something else very strongly—her *emunah* (faith).

The doctors grimly told Ira and Alysia that their baby would probably not survive the day. Ira wanted to be sure that Alysia would have the opportunity to see their baby. He whisked the baby to Alysia's side. One cannot fathom how Alysia and Ira felt then. Intense happiness at finding themselves with their baby at last and horrific sadness at what could be their baby's last day.

As unprepared as Ira and Alysia were for this situation, they were enabled to face this challenge with superhuman strength. They drew upon the immortal reservoir of *emunah* and *bitachon* (hope) inculcated in them since their own beginnings.

Tehila survived that first day and continued to grow over the months that followed. As she confronted challenge after challenge, tests and hospital stays that would have weakened giants, Tehila triumphed over the odds and is now a beautiful toddler with rosy round cheeks, penetrating eyes and a smile that could launch a thousand ships. Anyone who beholds her is enchanted by her charming personality and inevitably becomes inspired by her courage.

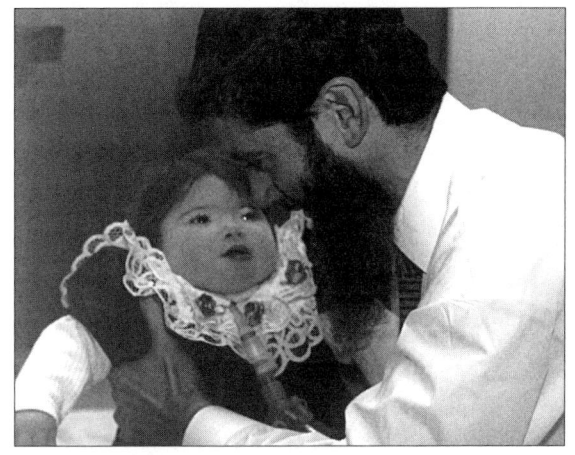

*Rabbi Goldwasser holding Tehilla Heller.*

One may ask in whose *zechus* (merit) has all this happened? Is it her father, Ira, a gifted musician and composer, a *chazzan* who serves his community with distinction and has inspired and uplifted thousands with his G-d-given talents and soul-stirring melodies? Is it in the *zechus* of Alysia, an absolutely dedicated young mother, an eloquent spokeswoman for the cause of humanity? Or is it in the *zechus* of Tehila herself? Tehila is one of those exalted *neshomos* (souls) who have come to this world to teach the lessons of life, and to make this a better world.

The literal translation of Tehila is "praise," because all who see her, praise her and especially praise the One Above for giving us this precious bundle of joy.

Pottersville, New Jersey

# THE TENTH MAN

*"Do not separate yourself from the community."*

—Pirkei Avos *2:5*

In the late 1700's, there was a certain man who did not join with the rest of the community. He did not attend the synagogue, nor did he participate in communal gatherings. The great Rabbi of his town paid him a surprise visit at his home one day. The man wondered why he was privileged to receive a personal visit from such an honored guest. The Rabbi came into the home and sat down by the fireplace. In silence, the Rabbi took a stick and separated one of the glowing coals from the fire. He sat the entire time and watched the coal until it completely went out. Without saying a word, the Rabbi got up from his seat and left the house.

The unspoken words shouted volumes.

# THE
# TENTH MAN

In the minds of jaded, big city dwellers, the small town is idealized as a utopia, far removed from the often harsh, urban existence. For city people, small towns often conjure up a relaxed lifestyle and the warm feeling of community often absent from urban settings.

When it is an ethnic small town, there is a deep and genuine close-knit feeling—an intensified peace of mind. The shared consciousness, the common goals, and the universality of daily lives creates the perception, as well as the reality, of belonging. The strong sense that every person is a significant cog in a large, complex mechanism is a daily feeling. Without that small, perhaps seemingly insignificant part, the whole mechanism cannot function.

Pottersville, New Jersey, in the 1950's, was a thriving Jewish farming community. European Jewish immigrants, who had traveled from small farms in Poland and Russia, settled there to raise chickens, operate milk farms or open small stores on Main Street.

There they raised their families, and as the years went by, Pottersville became a robustly-populated and warm Jewish community.

Over the years, however, the big cities became magnets for young people who wanted to continue their post-secondary Yeshiva education. Similar to many farming communities all over the United States, the second and third generation no longer chose to remain "on the farm." Sadly, Pottersville began to lose its luster as a vibrant Jewish neighborhood. *Shuls* (small synagogues) began to close, yeshiva enrollment dwindled and dried up, businesses folded. Before long, the small town in New Jersey was only that—a small town almost bereft of spiritual vitality.

I say "almost" because, as in many other dwindling locales, there are always people left behind who will not or cannot leave. Manny* was one such person. When his father retired, he took over the family business, a factory that manufactured metal bolts for industrial use. Manny's children had married and long since moved away, and when the family got together it was usually at his children's homes in Brooklyn and Long Island. They did not relish the long trip to Pottersville. They found the atmosphere in Pottersville stifling and depressing. The sight of the boarded up shul, that once reverberated with the stirring sounds of a congregation fervently singing their prayers in unison, simply crushed their souls, they said. Manny related the following:

"My children repeatedly tried to convince me to sell the business and move out, but I refused. I remained in Pottersville, committed to my work and bound by paternal loyalty. I just couldn't leave my father who was eighty-seven. Then, as is the way of the world, that day came and my father passed away. After the *shivah*

---

* The names in the story have been changed to protect the identities of people involved.

236

(seven days of mourning), quite naturally, I wanted to say Kaddish for my father's soul. Until now, maybe I had not been all that scrupulous about praying with a *minyan* (quorum of ten men) during the week. After all, of the few Jews who remained in Pottersville, not many were so religious as to conscientiously attend *minyan* every day. Everyone was on his own schedule. So most of the time I prayed at home.

"Only now I *needed* a minyan, and I needed one *every* day. I managed, by calling around, to get together nine men, including myself. I realized that I would have to go out into the streets of Pottersville to look for the tenth man. I knew it was ridiculous and probably fruitless; after all, I knew every Jew who was still left in town. Why did I think another person would suddenly materialize?

"Well, I remembered learning that every person must make his *hishtadlus* (maximum effort), so I went into the street and looked everywhere. Suddenly, I saw a man—he must have been seventy, dressed simply in jeans, a parka with a peaked hunting cap perched on his head—walking toward me. I stopped him. I knew it was a long shot, but I asked him, 'Tell me, are you Jewish?' The man nodded. He didn't even ask why I wanted to know so I prodded, 'We need you in the synagogue for a quorum of ten men to pray. You would be the tenth man.' The man looked at me skeptically. 'How can I be the tenth man? I don't know how to pray. The last time I was in a synagogue was at my *Bar Mitzvah*. You know how many years ago that was? What little Hebrew I knew then, I've long forgotten. I'm worthless to you as a Jew.'

" 'Fella,' I said, 'I must tell you, there is no such thing as a worthless individual. You happen to be a valuable commodity. Because, although you don't know the words, your physical presence alone is enough. All you have to do is stand there while we pray and you've fulfilled your function.'

"The man seemed embarrassed, but after a little more coaxing, he reluctantly came into the synagogue. All the other members of the *minyan* were relieved when they saw me with another man in tow, and someone quickly offered the newcomer a *siddur*. He refused, saying, 'I don't need one' and walked to the back. He stood throughout the service, his hands folded in front, his posture erect, his shoulders thrown back like a soldier on duty. The expression on his face was serious, but he seemed insouciant and blasé, as if the proceedings had little to do with him.

"Every day following this, for weeks that became months, I would go out into the street right before *davening* and bring Herb—that was his name—inside. He would never enter the *shul* as if he belonged there. He always made it look as if he just happened to be passing by. And, every day, he would take up the same position in the back of the synagogue with the same earnest expression, the same guarded posture—he would not even take a seat.

"To tell the truth, I began to take him for granted. I just always knew I would go out and find him there. Then, one day, almost at the end of the year of mourning for my father, I went out to get Herb and he was *not* there. I looked down the street. Maybe he was delayed, someone offered. Someone else suggested that perhaps he was in Florida. But I knew that couldn't be the case. I knew that despite Herb's air of indifference, he had realized how important a role he played. He knew he had become a part of the group—a critical part of the group. He would never miss a day unless something had happened to him. I began to inquire in some of the stores if they knew where Herb was. I chided myself for not getting his address and telephone number after all these months. Following a short investigation, I found someone who knew Herb. He told me that

Herb had suffered a severe heart attack and was in the intensive care unit in the local hospital. I wasn't surprised, since I had felt all along that Herb was committed to the *minyan*. I knew he would never miss it unless he were physically unable to attend.

"I rushed over to the hospital and was directed to his bed in the intensive care unit. He was in a semi-comatose state. Herb's eyes were closed and there were tubes and wires coming out of his arms and chest. His face was oddly flushed and I felt saddened at his debilitated state. I realized how much a part he had become of our little Jewish community, although he had never even opened the prayer book. 'Herb,' I called, 'It's me! How're you doing?' The nurse who was adjusting his I.V. said kindly, 'He can't hear you. He isn't conscious.'

"I stood a few more minutes in front of Herb's bed and then turned to leave. I spun around swiftly when I heard rustling behind me. Herb had opened his eyes wide and was looking at me. He lifted his index finger a few inches from the mattress and called out excitedly, 'Manny, *minyan?*' Herb then closed his eyes for the last time and returned his soul to his Maker."

## San Antonio, Texas

# THE ALAMO

*"Children's education must never be interrupted, even to rebuild the Temple."*

—Talmud Shabbos *119B*

*There is a traditional story told about the Baal Shem Tov, the founder of Chasidism. It seems he used to travel in a most peculiar way. Instead of facing the road, the driver of the Baal Shem Tov's wagon faced his passenger sitting inside. The horses' reins would be over his shoulders and the driver would hold them in his hands. Wherever the horses took the Holy Master, the Baal Shem Tov, would be considered Divine Providence, since whenever the Baal Shem Tov was in a particular place at a particular time there was always an important reason.*

*So, too, in life we can never know why we end up in a particular location or why we meet certain people and experience certain situations. To be sure, nothing is by chance—everything is Divinely decreed. The autumn leaf that gently falls from the tree to the ground lands on a particular side because of Providence. As we move through each day in this earthly world, we should always keep in mind that the material and the spiritual are ultimately one.*

# THE ALAMO

It was early July and I had been flown to San Antonio, Texas to
give a series of talks to teenagers gathered from various south-
western cities. The program was going splendidly and I especially enjoyed what turned out to be a motivated group of young
people. It was Friday and, in the afternoon, the organizers had
scheduled a visit to the Alamo. However, the event organizers were
in a quandary as to whether the program should be canceled—there
was a heat wave and the local temperature had already risen to one
hundred degrees. Some of the organizers thought it would be dangerous to take the participants outside for any length of time in such
extreme weather. However, for some strange reason, although the
majority voted not to go, we found ourselves going through the
entrance of the historic Alamo. The young people entered singing
one of the spirited Hebrew songs that they had learned at our program.

As we made our way, I noticed a middle-aged couple following our group, observing our every step. I could sense their curiosity about something; however, I knew not what. Finally, the couple approached me and began, "We just moved to Texas. We have two young children and have decided not to enroll them in any type of religious school. Religion, we feel, is not for the new generation. It's archaic and will not appeal to them. We felt there wasn't enough liveliness and meaning for young people to relate to. However, in watching your spirited group of teenagers, their enthusiasm and their obvious delight in spirituality, we're not so sure that we have made the right decision."

I spoke to this couple for quite some time, both at the Alamo and then later, long distance, by telephone. Eventually, they began to slowly introduce a dimension of spirituality into their home which in their words "changed their lives for the better." A trip to the Alamo, a trip to the grocery, waiting at a bus stop—one never knows. Like the wagon driver of the Baal Shem Tov, we were in the right place at the right time.

This couple just needed to witness some enthusiastic and lively young spirit in Judaism to reconfirm their Jewish identity and share this with their children.

# London, England

# CANDLELIGHT

*"There shall be no strange god within you."*
—Tehillim *81:10*

*"G-d shall not be a stranger to you!"*

—*Rabbi Moshe of Kobrin, Russia, 19th century*

The problems of missionaries and cults are not new. Decades ago, in Europe, a man traveled from a small town to Rabbi Shimon of Skanowitz. He was despondent and recounted how his daughter had not received a proper education and was now living in a convent, prepared to convert to Christianity. As the man continued his story, he explained, with a broken heart, that his daughter had grown up without any friends in their small town. She had been befriended by missionaries, who were now persuading her to convert. The Rabbi asked immediately for the location of the convent. He called for his personal attendant, asked for his hat, coat and boots and set out in a winter storm to the convent.

Once he reached his destination, the Rabbi stood on the street corner and penned a note to the young lady at the convent. It said, "I, Shimon of Skanowitz, am waiting for you." He specified the exact street corner in his note, folded it and gave a few pennies to one of the local children to smuggle it into the convent. For the entire day the Rabbi waited for this young woman. Soon snow began to fall heavily. After a while both the Rabbi and his attendant were knee deep in snow. They waited throughout the entire night for a sign of this young lady. Neither the Rabbi nor his attendant moved from their spots. If one left for a few minutes when necessary, the other would remain.

By dawn, the attendant said to the Rabbi, "It seems as though she is not going to appear. Isn't it time to go home?" The Rabbi would not hear of it. The second day passed, the snow continued to fall and still there was no sign of the young lady. It was now the third day. By this time the temperature was sub-zero, yet the Rabbi wouldn't contemplate leaving. On the third night, all of a sudden, the Rabbi and his attendant saw a shadow emerging. A young woman ran towards them. When she reached the Rabbi and his attendant, she identified herself as the young lady to whom the note was addressed. Rabbi Shimon asked her, "Why did you finally come to me?" She answered, "Rebbe, I knew that you would never leave without me."

# CANDLELIGHT

One of my most heart-wrenching experiences occurred when I was asked to testify on behalf of a mother in the Midwest whose child had been kidnapped into a cult. It was the child's father who came to me. The mother had been involved with and had witnessed the horrors of the cult firsthand. Now, with her daughter trapped in the cult, she felt as though her own daughter was being turned against her.

I will never forget describing to the judge in the custody battle the common practices of cults. These practices include sleep deprivation, high sugar diets, constant brainwashing, mind control, etc. Cults manipulate people, require total commitment and punish any questioning of doctrine. Many demonize family members and control all aspects of life. Naturally, the leader of these groups is above reproach. After many trying hours of discussion and deliberation, a judgment was handed down in favor of the mother. The child would be given a chance to live life with her soul and mind intact.

I was reminded of this incident later when I was consulted by a couple living in England. They explained that their son Steve* had become entangled in a cult. He was now totally alienated from his family. They kept waiting for him to snap out of it. However, when Steve had last come home, he no longer called them Mom and Dad, but instead referred to them by their first names. The parents then realized that his last remnant of respect for them was gone.

The parents also informed me that Steve would sit for hours at home watching a video of the cult leader delivering a sometimes unintelligible, endless diatribe. Their son, they said, used to be a gregarious, popular boy. He had had many friends, was quite athletic, and had enjoyed the arts. Now, the entire focus of Steve's life was the cult. His friends had slowly disappeared. When Steve would come home, it was always the same robotic discussions. His eyes appeared to be somewhat glazed. The parents cried to me. Something drastic had to be done; they knew not what.

After taking down information about Steve, his family and the particulars of the group that he was caught up in, I asked my usual question, "Is there spirituality in the home? Are any of our precious Jewish traditions observed?" There was a moment's hesitation. "We tried when we first got married, but with all of today's pressures, things were just too hectic. We never got around to it."

After I heard this answer, for some reason, which I still cannot fathom even today, I asked the couple if they would consider lighting Sabbath candles. Perhaps I thought that the glow of the candles would spread a positive aura of holiness in the house and light up the prevailing darkness. As our great Rabbis have taught, a little bit of light dispels much darkness.

It was a couple of months before Steve came home again. Steve

---

* The names in the story have been changed to protect the identities of people involved.

252

happened to walk into the dining room upon his arrival Friday night and was startled to see two shining candles. He asked his mother, with intense interest, why she was lighting candles. She explained that she had introduced this sacred tradition into their home, and she told Steve all that she could remember of what I had told her about the significance of lighting the Sabbath candles.

During the many months of Steve's involvement with the cult nothing had made an impression on him—neither his parents' logic nor their screaming, and certainly not the people his parents had summoned to try and talk with him. But there was something about the holy glow of those candles that seemed to penetrate the outer shell of his inner being. He asked his mother where she had learned about it and she told him it was from a Rabbi they had consulted. Steve listened intently to what his mother was saying. Two days later, on Sunday at approximately two o'clock in the afternoon, I received a call from Steve himself. In a long conversation, which covered many different topics of spirituality and human interest, we began to establish the beginnings of a rapport. Steve informed me at the end of the conversation that he was going to leave England to visit the States during the next month. I immediately invited him to New York to continue our discussion in person. During this interval I researched the cult which Steve was caught up in. I worried whether I would have the right words to say to this clearly anguished soul who had wandered so far from his roots.

October twentieth came a lot quicker than I expected. I first met Steve at my office in the city. After a brief greeting, we immediately continued our discussion that had started by phone. I only wish I had kept a detailed diary of our discussions and meetings. After the end of each discussion, I felt absolutely drained, for I tried to access every bit of spiritual energy that I possess to open new windows in

Steve's heart and soul.

Three weeks later I finally felt that our discussions were definitely progressing. Steve was beginning to discover new territory that had generated in him a tremendous amount of interest and curiosity. He had begun to sincerely analyze his position and the possibility of re-attaching himself to his ancestry. Because of all this I invited him for the Shabbos dinner. I asked him to come the following Friday night. To my surprise, Steve readily accepted. The Shabbos meal was going perfectly. Steve enjoyed the singing, the Torah discussions and the delicacies that had been prepared in honor of the Shabbos. It was indeed a charmed evening.

Then it happened. The doorbell rang. We were not used to hearing the loud chime of the doorbell invade the tranquility of the holy Sabbath. Immediately, thinking that it must be an emergency, I bolted to the door. A messenger stood there asking for Steve by name. He handed Steve an envelope and disappeared. The contents of the envelope included an airline ticket and a considerable amount of cash. There was also a letter from the leaders of the cult telling Steve how much they missed him; how much they loved him and wanted him to use the ticket and money to return immediately. Steve looked at me for a reaction. I was shocked. Questions raced through my mind. How did they know where he was? Why were they willing to expend so much effort to get him back? What impact would such a startling gesture have on Steve?

*Boruch Hashem* (thank G-d) this story has a happy ending. Steve never returned to the cult. He continued his search into his roots and eventually ended up in Israel. He studied in a yeshiva in Israel where he still lives to this day. I think about this incident time and time again. What has always bothered me is the following: Look at how far that missionary group was willing to go to *capture* a *neshomoh* (soul). How far are *we* willing to go to *keep* a *neshomoh*?

To be sure, it is our responsibility to give of our time and resources to effectively reach out and bring back those who have become alienated from their roots.

Rabbi Moshe Feinstein, who was one of the foremost *halachic* authorities of our generation, once stated that just as it is a *mitzvah* to give one-tenth of our income to charity (*ma'aser*), so too it is a mitzvah to contribute one-tenth of our free time to *klal* work (work on behalf of the community).

In fact, Rav Nosson of Nemerov composed a special prayer to be said each day on behalf of all those who have lost their way to Judaism.

# Shannon, Ireland

# A VOICE OF HOPE

*"'Days are coming,' says Hashem, 'and I will send a famine to the land. Not a hunger for bread, nor a thirst for water. Only to listen to the word of G-d.'"*

—Amos *8:11*

# A VOICE
# OF HOPE

very year around 3,500,000 people visit Ireland. Recently, I
was one of them. Most of the tourists came from Great
Britain and the United States. A majority of the tourists
were descendants of the millions of Irish people who emigrated to
the United States at the beginning of the twentieth century. Other
visitors come because of the low cost of touring, good highways,
charming rural landscape, and historical attractions. I found myself
in Ireland for none of the above reasons; rather it was simply a
stopover on my way to Eretz Yisroel (Israel). According to Jewish
tradition, everything in our lives is *hashgacha pratis* (Divine
Providence). Every stop we make along the road of life is Divinely
decreed. It is often beneficial to pause at various stations in our life,
to consider our purpose and mission and we may be surprised at
how interconnected are certain aspects of our lives.

I couldn't possibly imagine what my connection could be to
Shannon, Ireland. I was interested in some of the special green flow-

ers that the local Irish were displaying at the airport. In fact, I was asking where these flowers came from when a young man in his early twenties approached me.

"Excuse me, sir. Could I ask you a question? After hearing your voice I thought perhaps you were Rabbi Dovid Goldwasser from the morning radio program hosted by Nachum Segal." Astonished, I turned to the young man and answered, "Yes, I'm Rabbi Goldwasser." The young man explained that he was an American tourist from Rochester. He said he had drifted so far away from Judaism that there was little he could remember, if anything at all, about his heritage. However, one morning he awoke earlier than usual. To pass the time until his classes began, he turned on the radio to see if there was anything worth listening to. While fumbling with the radio dial he hit 91.1 FM. There he heard Nachum Segal's morning radio broadcast, during which I have the privilege of giving a five-minute talk on various topics of interest to the Jewish community.

There was something about the program which made an impression on him. He found himself listening to the program with more interest than he could have ever imagined. Perhaps his soul was experiencing a famine that his body was not aware of. After the program, memories of what he had heard remained in his mind throughout the day. Before he went to sleep that night, he set his alarm so that he would be up in time to listen to the show. This time, with pen and paper in hand, he took notes on what was said. In no time, he became an avid listener. Little by little he took concrete steps to reconnect with his heritage. Soon he had progressed in his studies and development in *Yiddishkeit* (Judaism) to the point where he decided to continue his studies in the place where hundreds of thousands have flocked in search of their heritage—*Eretz Yisroel*. He told me he had always wanted to call the radio station and thank us for being the catalyst that began his journey home. *Hashgacha pratis* saw to it that he had his chance.

*Renowned radio personality Nachum Segal (right) at work in his studio with Rabbi Goldwasser.*

# Rockland County, New York

# HEAVENLY DEFENSE

*"Angel, oh angel,*
*You're an angel,*
*Be it so.*
*But is it really remarkable*
*To be an angel?*

*You're in heavenly heights.*
*You don't have to eat,*
*You don't have to drink.*
*Children you don't have,*
*Income doesn't worry you.*

*Contrawise, angel oh angel,*
*Come down on earth to us,*
*Be also in need of food,*
*Be also in need of drink,*
*And be a parent of children,*
*Then we will see*
*Whether you're really an angel."*

*—Rabbi Moshe of Kobrin, Russia, 19th century, Ohr Hachasidim*

The cemetery represents a variety of things. Some people receive solace and comfort from being there. Others are too terrified to even venture near its entrance. The cemetery has a sanctity and an aura all its own. There is an other-worldly character there—it is inhabited by those who have passed on to eternal life. Although they are no longer a part of this world, they are buried in the land of the living.

Jews strongly believe in the hereafter. We know that humans have been charged with a special mission in this world to follow a righteous path. Upon the successful completion of our mission, we are rewarded eternally in a manner beyond human comprehension.

Those souls who have passed on will continually have a connection with family, friends and followers who have been left behind. We, in turn—at various times in our lives—pray for them, do good deeds in their memory and feel a strong sense of communication with these departed souls.

It says in the books of Kabbalah (Jewish mysticism) that sometimes we have difficulty going to sleep—not because of insomnia—but, rather, because during the time of transition from the conscious state into sleep (the "Twilight Zone") there are souls trying to contact us. When we perceive them, this startles us and we wake ourselves up.

It is an ancient Jewish tradition to pray by the gravesite of tzaddikkim (righteous people). By doing this we wish to evoke their merits and to be blessed and protected by G-d for their sake. Indeed, the Talmud (Brachos 7) states that "the righteous, in their death, are called living."

On my travels throughout the world, I always visit the graves of the righteous in both famous and lesser known cemeteries. The feelings and inspiration that I derive from those visits bring profound meaning into my life.

# HEAVENLY
# DEFENSE

I t was an extremely difficult day for Ron Newman*. His lawyer had just advised him that the case against him in court was, unfortunately, not going in his favor. Ron was accused of illegal business practices and, as he digested the magnitude of his high-powered attorney's words, he realized that in a short period of time, he would not only be penniless, but the business career and reputation he had spent twenty-five years building would be in ruins. As he drove down the highway toward his home, Ron was dazed. How was it possible? He had never done anything wrong—he had committed no crime, yet, due to a strange twist of fate, he was headed to suffer an unbearable future.

As Ron repeatedly reviewed the case against him, he noticed a group of people standing in a cemetery just off the highway. He had never given the cemetery much thought, although he had probably passed it thousands of times. Perhaps now, as he felt part of his free-

* The names in the story have been changed to protect the identities of people involved.

dom slipping away, he allowed himself to take notice and think about the non-physical, the esoteric. Curiosity stirred within him. What were these people doing? Why were they assembled in a cemetery in the middle of the day? He could see that it wasn't a funeral procession. Without any further thought, he impulsively drove his car to the cemetery gate toward where the group was standing.

Ron got out of his car and walked over to one of the men standing in the group. They all wore long black wool coats and dark hats with wide brims. "Excuse me," he said. "Can you tell me what's going on? Are you having some kind of meeting here?"

The man turned around and answered, "No, today is a special day for us. We are followers of the great, righteous spiritual man, the Skulener Rebbe, who is buried here. When we lost him, our guiding force and best friend was gone forever. Today is his *yahrtzeit* (the anniversary of someone's death). We've all come here today to pray for both his soul and for our souls."

"And what brings you here?" the man then asked Ron.

For some reason, when Ron heard this man's question, the floodgates burst. He did what he had never done before. He disclosed to a complete stranger the details of his untenable situation and the case threatening against him in court. The man, who had by now introduced himself as Sol, listened with compassion and understanding as Ron recounted this story.

When Ron had concluded, Sol advised, "Actually, when we visit the Skulener Rebbe's grave, it's a time when we pour out our troubles and express our sadness. We pray for solutions or answers, for Divine help. Perhaps you could try this and you too would be helped."

Truth be told Ron hadn't prayed for years, but he was willing at this point to do anything to alleviate his anxiety and feelings of foreboding. To Ron's surprise, as he began praying, he discovered that prayer is a powerful form of expression and no previous experience is necessary. On the day that might've been his lowest, Ron found himself standing with some fifty religious men dressed in black, all praying, some sobbing, at the grave of a righteous soul of whom Ron had never heard.

That night, as Ron went to sleep, he dreamt incredibly vividly. In his dream an elderly man with an undeniably holy and peaceful countenance appeared. This holy man instructed—no, commanded—Ron to use a different defense in court. He explained exactly what Ron's lawyer should say. Ron awoke, startled. Who was this holy man? What was this dream all about? Unable to fall back asleep, he spent the remainder of the night in his bed desperately trying to figure out the dream. He felt himself becoming overwhelmed with a sense of spirituality. Deep within, he had begun to sense that perhaps his course in life was about to change forever.

The next morning, he scheduled an early appointment with his attorney. Once inside the office, Ron began excitedly, "Mr. Shay, we've got to change our defense! This is how and what I would like you to do in court." Ron proceeded to relate the elderly man's words from his dream.

Once the lawyer had heard what Ron had to say, he responded, "This whole thing must be getting to you. The defense that you'd like to argue is crazy! It's legal suicide! I can't do it!"

Ron looked at his lawyer with the conviction that only a believer can have and said, "If you wish to continue to represent me, I'm afraid you will have no choice but to use this defense!" After a long discussion, Mr. Shay reluctantly agreed, but only because he and Ron had shared many years of a good working relationship.

Soon Ron had his day in court. Mr. Shay used the exact defense the holy man had demanded in the dream. To the astonishment and awe of all who had been following the case, Ron was completely cleared of all charges. His finances, his reputation, his career, his very being were left intact.

Jubilantly, Ron took his regular car route home. When he spotted the cemetery, he decided to search for a clue to the identity of the holy man in his dream. He easily found the grave he had visited only days earlier. Alone he waited trying to learn something about the holy man buried there. All of a sudden, a man came toward him, also intending to visit the grave. Ron was so excited to see him he attacked him with a barrage of questions: "Excuse me, can you please tell me about the man who is buried here?" The man gave Ron the Rebbe's exact name and other information. He also informed Ron that a *chossid* (follower) of the holy man lived in a nearby community. Ron wrote down the information, phoned his wife to inform her that he would be a little late that evening and sped off to find the house of the holy man's *chossid*.

Within a short time, Ron found himself at the Rebbe's *chossid*'s door. A young boy opened the door and invited Ron into the house. Ron turned pale and almost lost his balance when he saw a picture hanging on the hallway wall. He couldn't believe his eyes. The elderly man who had appeared to him in his dream was identical to the man in the large photograph on the wall.

Indeed, the righteous in their death are called living.

# GLOSSARY

**Aishes Chayil**—woman of valor.
**Aron Hakodesh**—Holy Ark.
**Avi Mori**—my father, my teacher.
**Bais Medrash**—study hall.
**Beis Din**—Rabbinical court.
**Bitachon**—hope.
**Bnai Yisroel**—the sons, or children of Israel; the Jewish people.
**Boruch Hashem**—thank G-d.
**Bracha v'hatzlocho**—blessings and good luck.
**Brachos** (pl.)—blessings.
**Chachomim** (pl.)—Sages, wise men.
**Chas V'shalom**—G-d forbid.
**Chasan**—groom.
**Chashmonaim**—Maccabean family that waged a victorious battle against the Greeks.
**Chasunah**—wedding.
**Chaverim** (pl.)—friends.
**Chazal**—acronym for Chachomim, *zichronom levrocho*—our Sages of blessed memory.
**Chein**—charm and grace.
**Chesed Hashem**—kindness of Hashem.
**Chesed Shel Emes**—loving kindness.
**Chevrah Kadisha**—Burial Society.

**Chizuk**—encouragement.
**Choshuvah**—important.
**Chumashim** (pl.)—Five Books of Moses.
**Chupah**—wedding canopy.
**Daitan alecha**—our thoughts are on you.
**Daven, Davening, Davened**—pray(ed).
**Din**—strict justice.
**Divrei Torah**—words of Torah or short Torah speeches.
**Dveikus B'Hashem**—clinging to G-d; a feeling of closeness with G-d.
**Emes**—truth.
**Emunah**—faith.
**Eretz Yisroel**—Israel.
**Erlichkeit**—honesty and authenticity.
**Gabbai**—attendant.
**Gematriya**—the numerical equivalent.
**Get**—Jewish divorce.
**Hakoras Hatov**—gratitude.
**Halachic**—according to Jewish Law.
**Hashgacha Pratis**—Divine Providence, Hashem's Divine intervention.
**Hashgachah**—Divine Providence.
**Hishtadlus**—effort, maximum effort.
**Hoshpo'oh**—influence.
**Ibergegebenkeit**—giving of one's self.
**Immi Morasi**—my mother, my teacher.
**Ir Hakodesh**—the holy city.
**Kabbalah**—mystical book.
**Kaddish**—a prayer said for the deceased.
**Kallah**—bride.
**Kavanah**—devotion.
**Kavod**—respect.
**Kedoshim**—martyrs.
**Kesher**—connection.
**Kesubah**—marriage contract.
**Kever**—grave.
**Kibud Av V'eim**—to honor one's father and mother.
**Klal**—the community.
**Klal Yisroel**—the community of Israel.
**Kochos** (pl.)—strengths.

**Kohen Gadol**—High Priest.

**Kristallnacht**—lit., night of broken glass; German pogrom of 1938.

**L'hagdil Torah U'lhaadirah**—to further intensify and glorify Torah.

**Levaya**—funeral.

**Ma'aser**—one-tenth of one's income to charity.

**Malach(im)**—angel(s).

**Maran Hagaon**—our master, the scholar.

**Matzav Ruach**—situation and atmosphere.

**Mazel Tov**—good luck, congratulations.

**Menorah**—a candelabra which was to be kept lit each day in the Holy Temple.

**Mesader kidushin**—the officiating rabbi.

**Mesiras Nefesh**—self-sacrifice.

**Middoh**—trait.

**Minyan**—quorum of ten men.

**Mishpocho, Mishpochos**—family, families.

**Moshiach Tzidkeinu**—the Messiah, our righteous one.

**Mussar**—the study of rebuke to improve one's character.

**Nachas**—pride; joy in someone else, especially one's children.

**Navi**—prophet.

**Neshomoh, Neshomos**—soul(s).

**Niftar**—passed away.

**Nisim**—miracles.

**Olam Habah**—the World-to-Come.

**Olam Hazeh**—this world.

**Paroches**—curtain.

**Pidyon Shevuyim**—redeeming captives.

**Posuk**—verse.

**Rachamim**—mercy.

**Rebbetzin**—a rabbi's wife.

**Ribono Shel Olam**—Master of the World.

**Seforim** (pl.)—Jewish books.

**Seudas Hoda'ah**—feast of thanksgiving.

**Shabbos**—the Sabbath.

**Shaliach**—messenger.

**Shechinah**—Divine Presence.

**Seforim**—Jewish books.

**Shivah**—seven days of mourning.

**Shlit"a**—acronym for *"sheyichye l'yamim tovim aruchim*—may he live for a good long life"; blessing for longevity.
**Shoah**—Holocaust.
**Sholom Bayis**—domestic tranquility.
**Shomayim**—heaven.
**Shul(s)**—synagogue(s).
**Siddur, siddurim**—prayer book(s).
**Simchah**—joy.
**Siyata D'Shmaya**—Heavenly assistance.
**T'noyim**—an engagement contract.
**Tayere**—holy.
**Tefillah, Tefillos**—prayer(s).
**Teshuva**—introspection.
**Tzaddik, Tzaddikim**—righteous person(s).
**Tzedakah**—charity.
**Yad**—pointer.
**Yahrtzeit**—the anniversary of someone's death.
**Yarmulka**—small cap worn by Jewish males to remind them that G-d is above them; lit., means "fear of the King."
**Yedidus**—friendship.
**Yeshiva**—religious Jewish school.
**Yeshua, Yeshuos**—salvation(s).
**Yeshuas Hashem**—G-d's salvation.
**Yevonim (pl.)**—Hellenists.
**Yiddishkeit**—Judaism.
**Yizkor**—memorial prayer.
**Yomim Noraim**—the High Holy Days.
**Zechus**—merit.
**Zt"l**—acronym for *"zecher tzaddik l'vracha*—may the righteous one be remembered with a blessing;" in blessed memory.